in practice

JOHN LEARMOUTH
Adviser for Physical Education
Metropolitan Borough of Calderdale

KEITH WHITAKER
Head of Peripatetic Physical Education Service
Metropolitan Borough of Calderdale

Designed by **Ideogram** Harrogate

Published by
Schofield & Sims Ltd. Huddersfield

Printed in Great Britain
by Butler & Tanner Ltd, Frome and London

contents

SEVEN DAY LOAN

This book must be returned on
or before the date stamped below

UNIVERSITY OF PLYMOUTH

EXMOUTH LIBRARY

Tel: (01395) 255331

This book is subject to recall if required by another reader
Books may be renewed by phone
CHARGES WILL BE MADE FOR OVERDUE BOOKS

Movement

0 7217 4515 6 ✓ 0035531

First printed 1976
Second impression 1976
Third impression 1977
Fourth impression 1978
Fifth impression 1981
Sixth impression 1984

foreword

It was with pleasure that I accepted John Learmouth's invitation to write a foreword to this concise, straight-talking book on educational gymnastics in the Primary and Middle school years. John Learmouth and Keith Whitaker, after many years' work with class teachers, students and pupils, finally decided to present for general publication a progressive plan of work for the logical and safe development of educational gymnastics in schools.

The book contains structured lesson material accompanied by teaching points and explanations. It is refreshing and reassuring to find that the authors are fully aware that gymnastics are based on certain clearly definable skills that will inevitably develop from the work sooner or later and that these must be clearly understood by the teacher and the children. Finish and polish are also unashamedly stressed.

For teachers and students with little or perhaps no background of physical education today, this book will prove invaluable. It reads well, is truly informative, and the photographs are a joy.

I can unhesitatingly recommend it as being an essential addition to the many books that have already been written on the subject. Its philosophy is educationally sound, its content clearly and simply stated and its presentation delightful.

Anne C. Gill
Adviser for Physical Education (Girls)
Gateshead

Every book on physical education aimed at the non-specialist teacher would seem to have as one of its objectives the easy preparation of progressive lessons using the material presented.

This book by J. K. Learmouth and K. Whitaker has been carried one step further. The presentation of simple themes and the form in which it is designed offer to primary school teachers opportunities to prepare a scheme of work without the obvious disadvantages of over-direction. At the same time, safety factors, teaching points and progression are emphasised.

An important feature of the book is the series of photographs showing good movement positions and demonstrating the ability of children in this age range. Again, these will be of particular value to teachers and students who have not followed a main course in physical education.

Since the abolition of the 11-plus examination in many areas, exciting developments have taken place in primary education. Teachers in primary schools in these areas have been involved in the introduction of French, modern mathematics, Nuffield science and team teaching. Modern building design and new materials have transformed primary education, and teachers are under increased pressure to keep abreast of the rapid changes.

In physical education the transformation took place many years ago and indoor lessons involving movement experiences and creative dance are well established. However, with increasing demands in other disciplines and the ever-present time factor, it is not always possible for the physical education courses in our colleges to equip teachers with sufficient knowledge and background to teach the subject efficiently.

The authors have these factors very much in mind and through their experiences with teachers at in-service courses they have developed their ideas to assist primary school teachers to overcome initial problems.

Experts, through their own enthusiasm and mystique, often perpetuate the myth that their specialism is sacrosanct. The authors are certainly not guilty of this and their book should be of interest to all primary school teachers, to students and to those responsible for the training of teachers.

G. E. Caine
Adviser for Physical Education (Men)
Liverpool

preface

It occurred to us that the presentation of material in this particular manner might demand some justification. For a variety of reasons, ranging from the nature of initial training to the number of new philosophies in new subject areas, it appears to us that there is a considerable number of teachers who feel the need for positive guidance in selection of lesson material, in the manner of progression in educational gymnastics, and in technical knowledge of the various movements that are likely to appear as children experiment with the ideas which are presented. We are sure that most of our colleagues in the Advisory Service will have experienced the situation in which, having presented a demonstration lesson as a very small part of a course of instruction, one sees one's lesson repeated over and over again in various schools, often to classes of widely differing age groups. The teachers concerned will have attended the course with the best will in the world but, not being specialists, have failed to understand how to put the principles of movement into progressive lesson form; they therefore grasp at the offered straw, the demonstration lesson, feeling that they have gained at least something from the course. Speaking for ourselves, as P.E. specialists, we freely admit that after three years of full-time training, we imperfectly understood the practice of these principles. The understanding finally came only after further study and experience. We suggest that teachers who have not received training in P.E. to at least main subject level are very much at a disadvantage when expected, as most of them are, to teach according to a philosophy they do not really understand. We have therefore set out to produce a series of progressions on given themes from which teachers may select activities around which lessons may be planned to cover a period of time. We offer reasons for undertaking such activities, and it is hoped that by following the various themes through a series of progressive lessons, teachers will connect these reasons and come to some greater understanding of the principles and practice of movement training.

The nature of the work, particularly in the earlier stages, tends towards the functional. This is quite deliberate, and we offer the following reasons. Firstly, there is a danger that, using the movement approach without a full understanding, the physically formative and corrective work will be neglected. It is our view that with young children it is very important to promote sound growth and to correct minor postural defects before they become permanent. Secondly, we feel that satisfying, creative work can be done only if a child can call upon a background of skills and ideas. Without these, creativity is inhibited by inability. In short, children cannot be expected to discover everything; they must at some stages be guided, and at some stages be taught. We hope that teachers will take every opportunity, throughout the entire scheme, to encourage creative and expressive movement, and the work is set out in a way that we hope will promote and make this easily possible.

The illustrations do not attempt to show every response to the stimulus of any of these. Neither is every photograph intended to suggest that this is what every child should do at the same time. The intention is to indicate the responses which tend to appear and which may be encouraged, and to show, via these photographs, the feeling for the aesthetics of movement that may be developed via the suggested work.

We have used the term 'educational gymnastics' throughout. The work could as easily have been described as 'movement' or 'movement training'. As the Bard said, 'A rose by any other name.....'.

J.K.L. and K.W.

Each thematic series has been produced with children of a particular age group in mind; thus **series 1** is designed to meet the needs of 5 year-olds in a reception class, and the final series to meet the needs and cater for the abilities of 12 year-olds. Whilst they are intended to be progressive, one cannot be definite about how long it will take to work through any one of the series, since the rate of progress depends upon a number of variables. It may be that having worked at a series for, say, four weeks, the teacher may decide that although only a third of the work has been covered it is in the best interests of the children to go on, or perhaps back, to another series for a while and return to the original series at some future time. It is not intended that teachers should work their way through an entire series, and then through the next, and so on. It is hoped that they will select material from a series on which to base a set of lessons. When the possibilities of this material have been exploited, they will then either select further material from that series, or material from another, on which to base another set of lessons. From our own experience, we have found that there is a year's lesson potential in each of the later series, but the children became bored by working the same theme for too long. Quite often we have found it desirable to use for a set of lessons material drawn from more than one series. Much of the work on a given theme will have an overlap effect on to another.

We therefore suggest that teachers should think in terms of a set period, say four weeks or half a term, select material from a series and plan the lessons for the period around that material. At the end of the period the teacher may review what has been done, and decide whether to carry on with further work from the same series or select from another for the next period. It should be borne in mind that in educational gymnastics there is nothing wrong with repeating the same basic lesson several times. The children need time to develop their ideas, to experiment and practise, and quite often the same activities should be presented for several consecutive lessons in order to ensure that the children have learned the things which the activities set out to teach; this makes progression possible. The apparatus used for such a lesson must be selected according to how each piece, or combination of pieces, can produce the type of work desired in terms of the theme being developed. There is no justification for using any piece of apparatus merely because it is there. This applies particularly to climbing frames. Clambering, hanging and swinging for discovery's sake is done at a very early stage, and as the children progress the frame will tend to be used less and less for climbing and more as a series of trestles from which other things are suspended. Isolated parts of the frame will be used to encourage more specific tasks to be undertaken.

It will be noticed that whilst the earlier series include Teaching points for every suggested activity, the later series do not. This is because **a** work in the later series tends to be merely a more sophisticated use of basic materials; thus there is little to say which has not already been said – the same Teaching points apply; and **b** it is hoped that having worked through the earlier series the Teaching points will become self-evident as the need for them arises.

We also hope that as a result of using this book teachers who have hitherto felt unable to do so will be enabled to devise their own series of lessons. There is no mystique in modern P.E. – it is all very straightforward. We have devised the series in this book by using the following simple formulae.

1 Select a theme (e.g. locomotion, balance etc.) or a combination of themes.

2 With a very simple instruction let the children experiment with it and discover the possibilities it holds for each individual.

3 Extend and develop the theme by asking for variations of any of the following elements of

movement – direction, level, speed, weight (light or heavy), smoothness or otherwise of flow. Extend the theme further by use of partner work.

4 Work the theme with use of apparatus, by the same methods as in 2 and 3.

lesson planning

We suggest that an acceptable standard form of lesson plan would be:

Introductory activity, in which the children are trained to start on some specific aspect of work as soon as they enter the hall, without being told to do so, at the start of every lesson. Some form of activity involving taking the weight on the hands is recommended, since confidence in this type of position is essential to progression.

Part one, movement and skill training on the floor.

Part two, the extension of part one work by the use of selected apparatus.

Closing activity, which will be similar in nature to the introductory activity.

use of apparatus

Having said that the apparatus work in part two should be an extension of the work in part one, we must say that with younger children, the level of skill and achievement one can reasonably expect in floor work is such that only very simple apparatus situations can be used in part two. This would appear to deny them the opportunity of using the more sophisticated apparatus, such as climbing frames, with which many schools are now equipped. Children of this age, however, have the physical and psychological need of opportunities for climbing, hanging, swinging, jumping, etc., that the larger apparatus gives. The teacher therefore finds herself in the position of knowing that she has a teaching task to do, in terms of basic movement skills, but realises that this alone will not satisfy all the physical and mental needs of the child. If, on the other hand, she concentrates on 'apparatus for its own sake', she is not really doing the teaching that is needed. It is suggested, therefore, that the two things be treated separately – i.e.

1 The educational gymnastics lesson, where aims and objectives in the skills of movement, on floor and simple apparatus, are pursued.

2 The large apparatus period, where the children are given the opportunity to climb, hang, swing, jump, etc., with the teacher placing only the simplest limitations on what the children do naturally. This is not a non-teaching situation, in that the skills of apparatus handling can be developed and maintained, as can the basis of group working and control. Needless to say, the layout and combinations of apparatus should be carefully planned, and should be changed as the children become more skilful.

The suggested ratio of lessons is:

	Movement Training	Large Apparatus
Reception	1	1
6 – 7 years	2	1
7 – 8 years	3	1

Obviously, the 3 to 1, or any other ratio, might not necessarily be achieved during the same week.

When planning for use of the large apparatus, the selection of which pieces are to be used and their position in the hall should be done with a particular class in mind. Obviously, there will be occasions when one class will be following another into the hall, and on these occasions the teachers concerned will find that out of, say, the seven pieces of apparatus available, perhaps four will be needed by both. In such cases, unnecessary handling can be avoided if the teachers find that certain positions for these pieces are convenient to both. In general terms, however, there is almost never an occasion when a complete apparatus layout which has been planned for one class will meet the needs of another, except for pure play – and this is not in itself physical education. At infant level, this type of lesson should be treated as a joint exercise in all the following: play; working as a member of a group; some apparatus handling; discipline (on whichever lines the school encourages); basic training for more objective use of large apparatus at a later stage; enjoyment; physical and mental development and the acquisition of skill.

Children should be trained and encouraged to handle as much of the apparatus as they can manage. They should also be made aware of the positive aspects of safety, e.g. landing mats placed under high apparatus. Generally speaking, young children will not attempt to do things of which they are not capable on large apparatus unless encouraged to do so – and what they construe as encouragement is often not what the teacher intended, e.g. drawing the attention of the class to a child who has climbed to the top of a climbing frame will often cause other children to think that this is what is needed to gain the teacher's approval.

Landing mats should be used under high apparatus as a 'breakfall' in case of accident, but they should also be used away from other apparatus as pieces in their own right.

The teacher's approach to this type of lesson must always be positive. Although she knows that the object of the lesson is mainly to let the children use the apparatus, some condition should be given to the children and the teacher should insist that they keep it in mind and try to carry it out. Such approaches as *Show me how many different ways you can . . . . .* are seldom productive for more than a few minutes. Simple conditions which insist on good quality landings, on showing certain positions on apparatus or in flight-off are more positive and more productive. If variety is being sought, an instruction such as *Do so and so. . . . Now do it a different way,* is a better approach.

Having used the first few lessons on free choice of apparatus to accustom the children to the various pieces, the teacher should have them work in groups. One group should work on each piece of apparatus until told to change. Completely free choice of working always leads to overcrowding, which can be dangerous, and queuing on the more immediately popular pieces, whilst others are unused.

As the children progress through the school, the conditions put upon their use of apparatus should become more definite in order to achieve given results, and later there will be opportunities to create some links between the large apparatus work and the current work in movement training.

This theme explores simple methods of moving about the floor. It is intended to lead the children to discover these methods, and to lay the foundation of good quality movement. Underlying the themes in the earlier series, however, is the sub-theme of space awareness. At this, the first stage, the children should be taught to make the best use of the available floor space. They should be encouraged when standing still to *find a piece of floor of your own*. When on the move, they should be taught to look before moving and whilst moving, and to keep clear of others. The children will need constant reminders, as suggested in the **Teaching points.**

The whole of this series is worked in free formation, i.e. the child selects his own place on the floor and moves freely without instruction regarding direction of movement other than that shown in the **Notes.**

1.1

Running, in any direction

Purpose

Awareness of floor space, i.e. forward, backward and sideways. Awareness of the presence, movements and space needs of the other children.

Teaching points

Use of eyes. The need to change direction to avoid others. Possibility of paths other than straight or curved, e.g. L-shaped, zig-zag.

Use your eyes as well as your feet.

Look to the sides as well as to the front.

Can you run a zig-zag path round the hall without touching anyone?

Notes

Children will tend to run in a circle around the hall.

At this stage, control and avoidance of collisions are first priorities. It is unwise to ask for variations of direction before this has been established.

At this point some of the foot remedial movements described in **appendix 1** could be included.

fig. 1

1.2

**Running, with contrasting qualities of weight, i.e.
i heavy running
ii light running**

Purpose

Experience of the feel of light movement, by contrast.

Basic concepts of control of movement.

Teaching points

In heavy running, the whole of underside of foot makes contact with the floor.

In light running, the heel never touches the floor.

For heavy running
Make a BIG noise with your feet.

For light running
Can you run so softly that I cannot hear your feet on the floor?

Which part of your foot does not touch the floor in light running?

Notes

Children will enjoy making a big noise with their feet and contrasting this with almost silent movement. Avoid the expression *Run on your toes.* Good quality movement on feet is almost always, except in ballet, achieved with the **weight high on the ball of the foot.**

fig. 2

1.3

Moving on feet, other than running

Purpose

To show that various ways of movement are possible with weight on one or both feet.

Teaching points

Explore the possibilities of hopping, skipping, jumping, galloping, rotating, double-foot hopping.
Can you hop on the other foot?
Can you move like this – heavily/lightly?
From jumps – land and squash down.

Notes

Whilst doing this, children will be jumping, and therefore landing.

Ask for **squashy** landings, i.e. a full bend at hips, knees and ankles, so that the bottom comes right down to the heels.

Having established this, you can then ask for **light** squashy landings, asking the children to try to avoid letting their heels touch the floor as they land.

N.B. It will probably be necessary to teach some children some of these movements.

fig. 3

1.4

Travelling on hands and feet

Purpose

To show that various ways of moving are possible with weight on hands and feet.

Teaching points

This can be done with *tummy looking at the floor* or with *tummy looking at the ceiling*.

Also with variety of hand and/or foot placement.

Can you do it with your tummy looking upward/downward?

It is harder to see where you are going in this position, so use of eyes must be first class.

Using hands and feet you can:
walk on all fours
do bunny jumps
move, turning over from tummy down to tummy up.

Notes

See figs 1, 2 and 3

Children are now adopting a bigger position, therefore each needs a larger share of the available space so the best possible use of space must be encouraged. This particularly applies to children getting close to the feet of others, where they might be kicked by the other child's heels.

Insist upon the qualities of light movement as established in **1.2**. It is very desirable for children to be encouraged to move in the crab or wrestler's bridge position, as shown in **fig. 3**.

Apparatus

Individual mats and/or hoops and/or skipping ropes

1a

Movement of apparatus

Purpose

Basic class organisation of apparatus movement. Groups (made up according to colour of shorts, or any other convenient way) should be formed to handle apparatus, since this is the way they will work with the larger apparatus later.

Teaching points

Space the articles sensibly on the floor. Ropes laid on floor to form either a straight line or a circle.

Which group can collect its apparatus nicely?

Can this group do it as well as that group?

Notes

At this point, the pattern of the future quality of apparatus handling is being established. No amount of time spent on getting this done well is time wasted. Think about how you will organise this, and have it done well. Tell each group to sit on, in or beside its apparatus until the class is ready.

1b

Running, using apparatus as obstacles
Stopping on mats, or in hoops or ropes

i **heavy running**
ii **light running**

Purpose

Creation of the concept of a link between floor work and apparatus work.

Teaching points

Necessity to use the eyes to observe positions of obstacles, as well as to avoid collisions.

Use your eyes.

Can you run without touching any of the articles on the floor with your feet?

Points as for heavy and light running.
Can you stop on the mat/in the hoop or rope?

1c

Moving on feet in a variety of ways, using apparatus as the limiting factor

Purpose

Continuation and extension of linking floor work to apparatus work.

Teaching points

Hop, skip, leap into, out of, over, or around hoops.
Hop, skip, leap into, out of, over, or around mats.
Hop, skip, jump over, or along ropes.
How lightly can you do this?
Can you do this using a curved/ziz-zag/L-shaped path?
Make your landings squashy.
When you land, let your bottom come right down to your heels.

Notes

Keep a close eye on landings and ensure that quality is maintained (squashy landings).

1d

Moving on hands and feet using apparatus as limiting factor

Purpose

Development of floorwork/apparatus work link, with the use of movements on hands and feet.

Teaching points

How lightly can you do this?
Can you do this using a curved/ziz-zag/L-shaped path?
Make your landings squashy.
When you land, let your bottom come right down to your heels.

1e

Replacement of apparatus

Purpose

To establish good habits of safety and care of both apparatus and facilities (not forgetting the floor!).

Teaching points

Only one person can put away his piece of apparatus at one time.
More haste, less speed.

Notes

It is better, at this stage, to tell each group, or even each child, when to move apparatus back to its place, rather than to allow a possible scrummage. Again, allow plenty of time for this and ensure it is done well. If it is, the time spent will be repaid with interest over years to come.

This series further explores simple ways of moving, and introduces simple balance positions. Then the two are put together to create simple movement sequences by moving from one position into another. Whilst doing this, the children are learning that the weight of the body can be supported on different parts (weight-bearing).

The intelligent use of floor space should be encouraged throughout the series, and constant reminders to *look for a space* and *find a space* should be given.

Further training in space awareness may be given by encouraging the children themselves to position the pieces of apparatus. Having done so, you should ask them to look at the positioning with safety, freedom of movement and consideration for the needs of others in mind, and to make any adjustments necessary. Apparatus should be kept clear of walls, cupboards, pianos and other projections or obstructions. In order to do this the diagonal arrangement indicated below is recommended. (**See plate A,** page 118.)

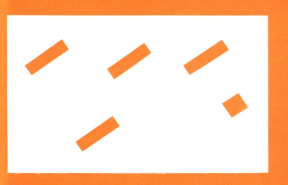

2.1

Running, in any direction

Similar work in series 1

Purpose

Maintenance of good quality movement.
First concepts of weight-bearing.

Teaching points

Which part(s) of the body bear(s) the body-weight
when standing,
when running?
Light running.
Use eyes as well as feet.

Notes

You are trying to establish the fact that, when
standing, weight is normally borne on feet; in running,
on one foot at a time. Foot remedial movements
(**appendix 1**) can be utilised as part of this activity.

2.2

Standing, on one foot and on two feet

Purpose

Establishment of the concepts of a given part bearing
the body-weight and of a different number of parts
bearing the body-weight.

Teaching points

The foot, or feet are small parts to take body-weight.
Which part of your body is bearing your weight?
How many parts are bearing your weight?
Let us call the small parts, such as feet, POINTS.

fig. 4

fig. 5

2.3

Balancing on points (small areas of contact)
See plate D (page 119)

Purpose

Establishing the concept that there are many
combinations of points of support which can be
used e.g.
two feet = two points, but also
one hand and one foot = two points
one foot and one knee = two points.

Teaching points

There are many possible combinations of two, three
or four points, e.g. use of points other than hands and
feet, such as head, knees, elbows.

Can you put your weight on two/three/four points?

*Can you show me a different position on the same
two/three/four points?*

*Can this be done with tummy facing floor, ceiling, or
side walls?*

Notes

See figs. 1 – 30

The number of points can be increased but more
than four at this stage tend to produce positions
which are neither aesthetically pleasing nor
physically useful.

Use of head, hands, elbows, knees and feet are the
points to encourage.

2.4

**Moving from a balance on a given number of
points into a different balance on the same or on
a different number of points**

Purpose

First steps towards a sequence of movement skills
newly acquired.

Teaching points

The children should be encouraged to make a smooth
and aesthetically pleasing transition from one
balance to the next.

Notes

The children should be helped to appreciate that this
is balance-move-balance.

fig. 6

series 2 part 1

Balances on two points

fig. 7

fig. 10

fig. 11

fig. 8

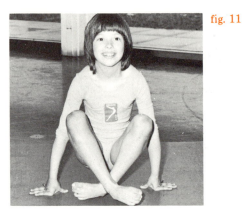

fig. 9

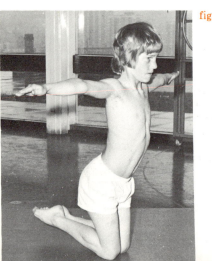

fig. 12

Balances on two and three points

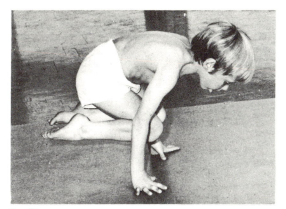

fig. 13

fig. 16

fig. 14

fig. 17

fig. 15

fig. 18

series 2 part 1

Balances on three points

fig. 19

fig. 22

fig. 20

fig. 23

fig. 21

fig. 24

Balances on three and four points

fig. 25

fig. 26

fig. 27

fig. 28

fig. 29

fig. 30

2.5

Balancing on patches (large areas of contact)

Purpose

Weight-bearing on larger surfaces.

Teaching points

Patches are the large weight-bearing areas of the body, e.g. bottom, back, tummy, shoulders.

How many points are on the floor?

Let us call the larger area a PATCH.

Can you take your weight on that patch with no points touching the floor?

Can you put your weight on a different patch?

Is it usually easier to balance on one patch than on one point?

Why?

Notes

See figs. 31 – 38

Start in a sitting position, knees raised, feet and hands on floor, giving four points and a patch.
The ease of balance on a large area of the body, as opposed to a small one should be made clear to the children. It is possible that a mathematical link can be established without being too technical about the theory involved.

fig. 31

2.6

Moving from a balance on points into a balance on patch(es)

Purpose

Leading the children to explore the different possibilities of balance and movement.

Teaching points

First position should flow into second. The obvious way to make the transfer is usually the best.

Can you go forward from your points to your patches?
ditto *backwards?*
ditto *sideways?*

Notes

The movement which links the first position to the second should be both functionally sound and aesthetically pleasing. Do not encourage ridiculous positions or transfers merely for the sake of finding a different way.

Examples of movements which may be used as a link between the first and the second balance are:

any type of jump – forward, backward or sideways

any type of rolling movement – forward, backward or sideways

any type of feet-hands-feet movement – bunny jump or simple cartwheeling movements.

2.7

Moving from a balance on patch(es) to a balance on points

Purpose

As for **2.6**

fig. 34

fig. 32

fig. 35

fig. 33

fig. 36

fig. 37

fig. 40

fig. 38

fig. 41

fig. 39

fig. 42

Apparatus

Benches and/or walking planks and/or boxes, stage units, or any other low but raised horizontal surface

2a

Movement of apparatus

It is wise to establish semi-permanent groupings for the handling of each piece of apparatus.

Similar work in series 1

Purpose

Establishment of procedures for handling large apparatus.

Teaching points

Apparatus is always lifted and carried, never dragged.
Which group can get the bench into position without my hearing it move?
Think where your piece of apparatus should be placed.

Notes

With most apparatus of the type suggested, one child to each corner is the best method of handling. Children are much more able to handle apparatus than we tend to think, (see **plate F,** page 120). Give them plenty of practice. Allow the children to select the position for each piece of apparatus, and then ask them to think about safety, mounting and landing space to ensure that their positioning is good, and alter it if necessary.

2b

Balancing on apparatus on points and patches
See figs. 39 – 46 for points balances.

Purpose

Extension of the concept of weight-bearing, already established on the floor, in a different situation, i.e. on apparatus. The introduction of balancing on surfaces which differ from the floor in texture and probably in contact area necessitates extensions of balancing techniques.

Teaching points

Can you show on the apparatus the positions on points that you showed on the floor?
Can you show them on patches?

Notes

With the amount of apparatus available to many schools it will not be possible to have the whole class on large apparatus at once. If this is so, have one group practising the activities on the floor, whilst another uses the apparatus.
In order to keep children on the move, thus avoiding bottle-neck situations, it is often wise to organise this activity on the basis of free movement from one piece of apparatus to another.

fig. 43

series 2 part 2

fig. 44

fig. 45

fig. 46

2c

Replacement of apparatus

Similar work in series 1

Purpose

To get children to recognise and remember the correct storage position of each piece of apparatus.

Notes

It is better if the piece of apparatus which has to be carried furthest is taken first. In the early stages, good habits will be learned if the second piece is not moved until the first piece has been returned to its storage position.

In this series, the work done on weight and bearing in **series 2** is extended to transferring the weight from one body part to another. The floor work is best done with the children in free formation – *find a large space for yourself* – and use of the eyes to avoid other children should be constantly encouraged. Space awareness, in terms of floor space, is not acquired quickly; constant reminders are necessary, and will be for some time to come. Good quality movement, particularly in running, should be sought. Children will still enjoy the contrast of light and heavy.

Apparatus should be at a low level, 40 cm being regarded as a maximum, in order to enable the children to work from floor to apparatus and from apparatus to floor without the complication of having to jump on and off. Some jumps off the apparatus might well appear in the course of the children's exploration of the theme, but such jumps should be from choice, rather than from necessity imposed by apparatus which is too high.

Positioning of apparatus should be suggested by the children, with careful prompting by the teacher. It should be kept clear of obstructions, e.g. walls, cupboards, etc. The diagonal type of layout is recommended. (**See plate A,** page 118.)

3.1

Various ways of moving on feet, in any direction, starting with running

Similar work in series 1 and 2

Purpose

Maintenance of good quality in simple movement.
Concepts of weight transference.

Teaching points

When you are running, you are putting your weight first on one foot, and then on the other foot.

How can you describe hopping?

How can you describe jumping?

Remember that we want LIGHT running.

Do not let your heels touch the floor.

Notes

Running can be described, in weight transference terms, as

left foot – right foot – left foot – right foot, etc.

or

foot – other foot – foot – other foot, etc.

Hopping, in these terms, is

foot – foot – foot – foot – foot, etc.

Double–foot jumping is

feet – feet – feet, etc.

These concepts should be put to the children continually, but quick understanding should not be expected.

3.2

Walking and running

Purpose

Concept of moving on points.

Teaching points

When you are walking or running you are moving on POINTS.

How many points are you using when you walk or run?

Notes

This is a difficult concept for a child to grasp. What the children are doing, in fact, is using two points, by transferring the body-weight from one point to another. Again, there needs to be much repetition of this, and patience in waiting for the concept to be grasped.

3.3

Moving on four points

Purpose

Reinforcement of the concept of moving on points.

Teaching points

Can you move on four points?

Can you move on a different four points?

Can you move on four points with your tummy looking up at the ceiling?

Can you move on four points with your tummy looking at the floor?

Notes

The best variations are those of level, i.e. with the body low, close to the floor, or high.

A true crab position is worth encouraging (see **fig. 3**).

3.4

Moving on three points

Purpose

As in **3.3**

Teaching points

Remind the children to **look** where they are going.

Notes

In response to the suggestion that they move on three points, children will usually use two hands and one foot. Do not ask for this to be varied (except by use of the other foot), since it is very difficult to hop on one hand.

fig. 47

fig. 48

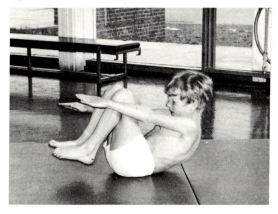

3.5

Weight transference; from feet to hands and back to feet
i   **on the spot**
ii **travelling around the hall**

Purpose

Formal introduction of concept of moving bodyweight from one part to another.

Teaching points

Feet − hands − feet movements can be in the form of bunny jumps, kicking horses, simple handstanding positions, simple cartwheeling movements.

Can you show a way of moving your weight from your feet onto your hands and back onto your feet?
Can you find space, and use your eyes more than ever?
Look behind you before kicking your legs up.

Notes

A crouch is a very good starting position. It is safe, and it is easy for children to get their weight on to their hands from this position.

Be watchful of children's spacing – they can easily kick each other.

If rudimentary handstands appear, tell the children to keep the head pushed back.

N.B. Cartwheel movements are really, in weight-bearing sequence, *feet – hand – hand – foot – foot,* but do not press the point at this stage.

The important thing is for the children to get the weight on to the hands.

3.6

Free movement, starting on feet and transferring weight to other parts

Purpose

To introduce rolling and other weight transferences.

Teaching points

If you are going to roll head over heels, start with your feet apart and look back through your legs.
Can you roll curled up in a tight little ball?
Can you roll in a long stretched position?

Notes

The object of this is to get the children rolling, either forward, backward or sideways in a curled position, or sideways in a stretched position. This will probably have to be suggested to the children. Do not be too technical about the weight transference involved, but do make the point that it starts as feet, hands, back of shoulders, and that at no point does the head touch the floor (**figs. 47 and 48**). There will be many interesting weight transferences attempted, no doubt, since this is a very creative situation.

fig. 49

Apparatus

**Benches and/or walking planks and/or boxes,
stage blocks and/or any other raised but low
horizontal surfaces**

3a

Movement of apparatus by groups

Similar work in series 1 and 2

Purpose

Continual reinforcement of principles of apparatus
handling.

Teaching points

Think where each piece should be placed.

Is it safe there?

Always LIFT, never DRAG.

Notes

Keep groups for apparatus as stable as possible.

3b

Movement on points, using apparatus

Purpose

This is the natural progression from the static work
on points in the previous series. It introduces the idea
that movement with apparatus brings possibilities of
new directions of movement, e.g. upward, downward,
in addition to the directions used on the floor. This
adds further dimensions to the concept of space
awareness.

Teaching points

Can you move on points on the apparatus?

*Can you move on points starting on the floor and
finishing on the apparatus?* See **Notes.**

Notes

The possibilities, according to the type of apparatus
available, are

1   from floor to apparatus
2   from apparatus to floor
3   along the apparatus
4   across the apparatus
5   over the apparatus
6   under the apparatus
7   through the apparatus
8   from apparatus to another piece of apparatus
    direct
9   from apparatus to another piece of apparatus via
    the floor.

3c

Moving on apparatus, transferring weight from one body part to another

Purpose

This is the progression and extension of **3b.** It is also the apparatus work related to **3.6**.

Teaching points

This is a matter of transferring the body-weight from one part to another. Children should be asked if they can reproduce their floor movements and use other movements on, along, under, over, across and through the apparatus;

from floor to apparatus

from apparatus to floor

from one piece of apparatus to another.

Notes

See fig. 50

The simplest way to start this work is by feet – hands – feet transfers. As it develops, other transferences of weight should be encouraged.

Rolls are possible on many pieces of apparatus, as are other points to patch and patch to points experiments, provided these were well covered in the floor work in part one.

If jumps from apparatus appear, ask for squashy landings, where children give at hips, knees and ankles as they meet the floor.

If apparatus is anything more than very low, landing mats should be used.

3d

Replacement of apparatus by groups

Similar work in series 1 and 2

fig. 50

Having used leaps, in **series 1** and **3**, as one method of moving on the feet, and encouraged sound landing principles, mainly for the children's comfort and safety as they meet the floor from the leaps, we now progress to extending the style and variety of leaping and making the landings more controlled. This both reinforces what has gone before and lays a firm foundation for what is to come later, when the children will be landing from greater heights and with considerably more forward speed to control. It is very important that the children should be encouraged to land without putting their hands to the floor. To do this, the back needs to be kept straight. If they land on their feet and allow themselves to topple forward on to their hands, there is a risk of injury, particularly to wrists, elbows and collar-bone. It is doubtful if such injuries would occur at this stage, but if a bad landing habit develops they might well occur later.

There are basically two types of controlled landing on feet; landing to **stop**, and landing to **rebound** (usually into another movement). The latter is not appropriate at this stage, since our predominant objective is to teach and encourage the children to control their movements. A landing to stop demonstrates that the child has controlled his movement, rather than allowed gravity or any other force to control it, where a landing to rebound is more likely to be the result of forces, rather than a deliberate and controlled action.

This is very much a teaching series, in that there is a set technique involved. There are, therefore, few opportunities for the children to use their own creative ideas. It might be considered that this series is best covered by dividing it into one or two lesson portions and spreading them over a period of time during which one of the more creative series is being covered.

All the activities in this series need the best possible use of the floor space. This is particularly so in part two, when the apparatus is in use. Children will need enough space to run up to the apparatus, pass over it, and land.

A diagonal placement of the apparatus is recommended, with the apparatus near the central line of the hall, so that children are not landing near walls or other obstacles or projections.

THIS

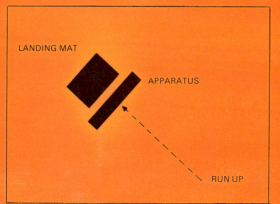

LANDING MAT

APPARATUS

RUN UP

not THIS

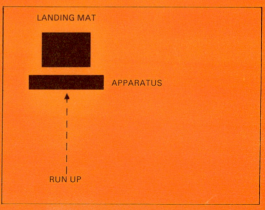

LANDING MAT

APPARATUS

RUN UP

4.1

Running, in any direction

Similar work in series 1 and 2

Purpose

Reinforcement of principles of good quality movement.

Teaching points

Do not let your heels touch the floor.

Light running.

Notes

Encourage movement paths other than straight.

Foot remedial movements (**appendix 1**) may be used as part of this activity.

4.2

Running, to high jump and landing on two feet

Purpose

Preparation for teaching landing techniques.

Teaching points

What do you have to do to get a light landing?
(Squash!)

What kind of landing do you get if you do not squash as you meet the floor?

Keep your hands off the floor.

What makes a landing soft and quiet?

Which parts bend as you meet the floor?

Notes

Here we are trying to get the children to identify the problems caused by the force of gravity, and to discover the physical solutions.

4.3

Standing jump, to land on two feet, to stop

Purpose

Formalising landing techniques for safety and
effectiveness.

Teaching points

Try to land without letting your heels touch the floor.

Bring your feet together before they meet the floor.

Keep looking straight ahead of you.

*Squash – then stand up straight and count to three
before you move away.*

Let your bottom come right down on to your heels.
See **fig. 51.**

Keep your hands clear of the floor.

Notes

As described at the beginning of this series, there are
two types of foot landing:

1 landing to stop
2 landing to rebound into another movement.

Whilst we need not clutter children's minds with this
information, the teacher must know which landing
she is asking for. 1 is the force-absorbing landing and
should be the first taught.

At this point, all landings should be to stop, since it
is very difficult to distinguish between a landing to
rebound and an uncontrolled landing where the child
rebounds because he cannot do otherwise.

It might be worth mentioning that the foot pattern
for jump and land in this way is from two on to two.
This ties in with the basic concepts of weight-
bearing. It may also be practised from one foot
to two.

fig. 51

Apparatus

Initially, individual mats or anything else (e.g. skipping ropes) which can be used as an object across which the children can move at a low level.

4a

Movement of apparatus (i)

Similar work in series 1, 2 and 3

Notes

Encourage sound handling techniques. Since the nature of work is different from the last series, ask children to reconsider best positioning of apparatus. Since leaping is involved, and therefore landing, draw attention to dangers from walls, projections, other apparatus, other children, etc., and position accordingly.

4b

Leaping across mat to land to stop

Purpose

Introduction of forward momentum as an additional factor involved in landing.

Teaching points

It is important that the head should not come forward/downward whilst landing. It should be kept in its natural line, and the trunk kept erect.

Make your landing squashy, etc.

Let your bottom drop until it almost touches your heels.

Notes

Leaps should be crossways over the mat. When accomplished well, let the children attempt leaps lengthways. These leaps may be performed from one foot to two, or from two to two. Do not ask for single-foot landings at this stage. Children must be strongly discouraged from letting the weight pitch forward on to the hands.

This is an activity which must be repeated over and over. Changes of method of practising may be made, but this theme is so important that it must be used until good landing habits are thoroughly ingrained. This particular activity may easily be included for a few minutes at a time when using other series and other themes.

If children have difficulty in avoiding pitching forward on landing, ask them to continue to squash but not to squash down as low as before. To control a landing where both downward and forward momentum are present, the landing posture should be slightly more erect, whilst still giving at hips, knees and ankles.

4c

Movement of apparatus (ii)
Benches, boxes, blocks, etc. to working positions

Teaching points

Is it safe to jump from your apparatus?
Is there anything in the way?
Is it far enough from the wall/cupboard/etc?

Notes

The teacher should check all flight paths and landing areas with safety in mind.

fig. 52

4d

Leaping from floor to land on apparatus, from apparatus to land on floor and from floor to floor, passing over apparatus

Purpose

Widening experience of landings, i.e. differing amounts of force and differing directions.

Teaching points

See fig. 52.

A stretched position should be shown in flight, followed by the squash on contact.

Make your landings squashy, etc.

Notes

Children tend to over-squash when first attempting landings from a downward jump. See that the give starts at toes and travels through ankles, knees, to hips, but is not over-stressed. Children should be encouraged to squash and then stand erect immediately, and hold the erect position before moving away.

This shows the teacher that they are really controlling the landing.

4e

Replacement of apparatus

Similar work in series 1, 2 and 3

Notes

If apparatus is being returned to storage one piece at a time, give the children something to do –
e.g. anything with weight on hands – whilst they are waiting, and when they have replaced their piece.

Locomotion and balance – use of shape

This series extends the children's movement experience by introducing positions and movements where the body is used in a given shape. It progresses by using changes from one body shape to another. It also invites the children to use rolls, but these should be treated as exploratory activities, provided they are safe. Teaching for good style is not yet appropriate. The forward roll is the one most likely to appear, and when children start to attempt it, they should be told to try to prevent the head touching the floor by pushing the chin down on to the chest. This avoids the child's whole body-weight being taken on the head, with the resultant stress on the neck.

Positions and movements where the feet are in a higher position than the head, even if only momentarily, should be encouraged. At the end of the series, the children are given the opportunity to connect movements one to another to create rudimentary sequences.

In part two there are times when work both on the floor and on apparatus is indicated. Although the nature of the work is fairly static, apparatus should be placed with the fact in mind that some children will be working on the floor around the apparatus. The diagonal apparatus arrangement is recommended, with the apparatus rather nearer the centre of the hall than if no floor work were involved.

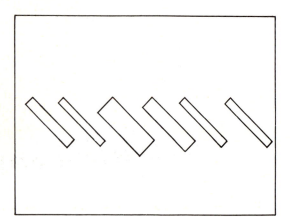

The balance principle which the children should learn is **the larger the base – the easier the balance.** In physical terms (ignoring the centre of gravity) the effect is as shown.

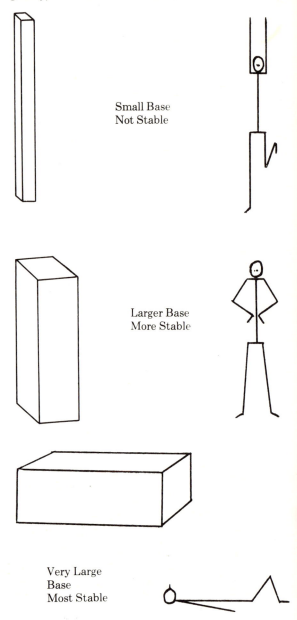

Small Base
Not Stable

Larger Base
More Stable

Very Large
Base
Most Stable

The base, in terms of a human body, can be
illustrated thus. Standing on one foot, the base can
be defined roughly as the rectangle a b c d.

Standing on two feet, the base becomes the
rectangle w x y z.

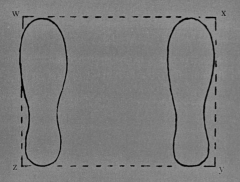

5.1

Running, in any direction

Similar work in series 1, 2, 3 and 4

Purpose

Repetition of quality work. Intelligent use of space. Formative work for feet and ankles.

Teaching points

Can you run without your heels touching the floor?

Use your EYES as well as your feet.

Light running.

Notes

Use of formative and corrective movements as in **appendix 1.** Vary the simple running with hopping on either foot or on both feet. Press for light quality.

5.2

Standing, showing LONG stretched position
Standing, showing WIDE stretched position

Purpose

Introduction of concepts of body shapes and sizes. Introduction of the concept that a large body shape may be narrow or wide.

Teaching points

When going for a stretched position everything (e.g. hands, fingers, feet) must be stretched to fullest extent:

try to touch the ceiling

be a giant

stretch your fingers.

Notes

Try to use the word to suggest the action – i.e. s-t-r-e-t-c-h rather than stretch.

Do not keep children in the stretched position for too long at each effort, but do correct individuals.

5.3

Stretch positions – long and wide, using different bases of support

Purpose

To cause children to realise that the same shape may be reproduced on bases other than feet.

Teaching points

Can you show this shape with your tummy looking at the floor?

. . . . . . ceiling?

. . . . . . wall?

Can you show this shape with your heels higher than your head?

Notes

Possibilities arising from these challenges are:

lying on front or back, crab position, side star position (**fig. 6**);

one hand and one foot, handstand against wall;

spanned positions on tummy and back.

5.4

Standing, going down to tight curled position

Purpose

Contrast between large and small body shape.
Control of movement which is gravity assisted.

Teaching points

Push your chin on to your chest.

As small as you can.

Make this a smooth movement all the way down.

When you are curled up, pull in tight.

Have you curled your hands?

Have you curled your feet?

Notes

Unless told otherwise, children will tend to drop to a crouch, with feet still on floor. It is better to encourage them to go right down kneeling, or lying on the floor on the back or side.

5.5

Showing a long stretched position then going into a tight curled position

Also going from a wide stretched position to a tight curled position. These may also be reversed.

Purpose

Introduction of concepts of changes from one body shape to another.

Teaching points

Try to avoid jerky movements.

Try to change your shape smoothly.

Sink down to the floor.

Make all parts of your body bend or curl.

Notes

The greatest emphasis should be placed on the extremes of stretch or curl. This will have a beneficial suppling effect on the spine and will in time make a greater range of movement possible.

5.6

Moving about the floor showing long and wide stretched positions

Purpose

These positions have been used statically. We now want the children to experience the positions in movement.

Teaching points

Can you jump and show a stretched position whilst you are up in the air?

Could you show a different stretch whilst in the air?

Can you show a stretched position whilst moving your weight from feet to hands to feet?

Could you roll in a stretched position?

Notes

When children are jumping, remind them of the squashy landings.

Children showing wide shapes in flight should be told to get their feet together before landing.

Rudimentary cartwheeling movements (**fig. 53**) will probably start to appear whilst the children are trying wide stretches whilst moving weight from feet to hands to feet. (See also **fig. 54** – a walkover.)

fig. 53

fig. 54

5.7

Moving about the floor showing curled positions

Purpose

Again, using positions whilst moving which have been established in stationary situations.

Teaching points

Can you move along the floor in a curled position – going forward?

. . . . – going backward?

. . . . – going sideways?

Try not to let your head touch the floor when you roll forward.

Notes

See figs. 47 and 48

Rolls will appear here as children move in a curled position.

Provided they are safe, there is little point in trying to teach rolling procedures at this stage. (**See Notes to 3. 6.**)

The tighter the curl, the easier rolling becomes.

5.8

Free choice of balances or positions on 1, 2, 3, 4 points or on a patch, allowing children to choose their own body shapes

See plate D (page 119)

Similar work in series 2

Purpose

To show that shapes may be varied by;

supporting the body on different parts,

changing the body position on the same base of support.

To extend the shapes concept by allying it to balance.

Teaching points

Can you show a stretched balance on points?

Can you show a curled position on a patch?

Can you show a stretched position on a patch?

Can you show a twisted stretch?

Can you show a twisted shape?

Can you change from a stretched shape to a twisted shape?

Notes

By allying the activities in this series to the balance work already done, further work may be done in the form of stretched balances, twisted balances etc.

series **5** part **1**

5.9

Floor movement, choosing from work done so far, to show stretched and curled positions whilst moving

e.g. moving from a stretch to a curl and back to a different stretch.

Moving from a stretch to a different stretch and finishing in a curl.

Showing a stretched position followed by a curled movement and finishing in a different stretched position, etc.

Purpose

To encourage children to use the ideas and skills they have been practising to create small sequences of connected movements.

Teaching points

Try to choose the best shape for each movement, but use both large and small shapes.

Possible movements are
jumping, rolling, turning over, rocking, twisting, cartwheeling.

Notes

Jumps will obviously be used during this activity. Landing principles – *stretch to land, squashy landings* etc. – should be remembered and, if necessary, revised.

The activities throughout this series may be further extended, and creative opportunities provided, by asking for variations and/or combinations of shape, e.g. spiky, twisted, twisted stretch, etc.

Many good stretched shapes may be obtained in bridged positions. The crab position, in fact, is probably the ultimate in stretching.

Apparatus

Benches and any other raised horizontal surfaces. If possible, a plain wall surface should be available. Landing mats adjacent to pieces of apparatus

5a

Movement of apparatus by groups

Each group to be responsible for its own apparatus

Similar work in series 1, 2, 3 and 4

Purpose

Formation of semi-permanent groups to be responsible for each piece of apparatus.

Notes

Ask children's opinions on best method of apparatus movement, placement etc.

The order in which pieces are moved from storage to working position is important.

5b

Showing a large balance position on the floor. Finding a place on the apparatus where you can show the same balance. Then showing a small balance position on the floor. Finding a place on the apparatus where you can show the same balance.

Purpose

Relating floorwork ideas to the apparatus situation.

Teaching points

The teaching points that should be used for all the apparatus work in this series are mainly those of encouragement, and asking children if they can produce variations of position whilst using the same base and the same shape.

Notes

The word 'balance' will here include any still position, but should mainly refer to a position above the apparatus, (i.e. not suspended). This is a fairly static activity and should therefore not be carried on for very long at one time.

5c

Stretched positions between two points of support

e.g. floor and apparatus; floor and wall; apparatus and apparatus

Purpose

Application of floorwork in a variety of different situations. Differences include planes, surfaces, levels.

Notes

See figs. 39 – 46

5c and **5d** are the apparatus version of activity **5.8,** and as stated in the **Notes** on that activity, the shapes may be varied by twisting, etc. Point out to the class that the positions they are working on are in fact balances, i.e. positions which are held for about three seconds.

5d

Stretched position between two points of support, then moving in a curled shape to a different stretched position between two points of support

Purpose

As for **5c.**

fig. 55

5e

Dismounting from the apparatus, moving in a stretched position to do so

Purpose

Further extension of shaped movement, using apparatus.

Notes

See figs. 55 and 58

Jumping dismounts will obviously be used. Continue to stress the necessity for squashy landings, and ask for lightness as the quality factor. **Figs. 56** and **57** are a sequence showing flight and landing from the same jump. Note the vertical line of the trunk as the feet meet the floor, the concentration, control and the commencement of the squash.

Children may also be encouraged to attempt dismounts where the weight is transferred from feet to hands to feet with the body in a stretched position.

Examples of this are
cartwheel off the apparatus **fig. 59**
handstand off the apparatus **fig. 60.**

fig. 56

fig. 57

fig. 58

fig. 59

5f

Replacement of apparatus

Similar work in series 1, 2, 3 and 4

fig. 60

The work on shape is developed to a point where the children are led to discover various principles of balance. These have practical applications in the child's management of his own body, and may well form a natural link with mathematical work done in the classroom (see below). Size is used as a variant to shape in both movement and balance, and comparisons of size are introduced as physical possibilities.

In part two, different heights, surfaces, etc., are used to extend the range of possibilities of use of shape and size, and new balance situations are created.

The degree of sophistication of ideas and the standard of performance will vary from the very simple to the advanced, depending on the age and movement background of the children. This series can with profit be used again and again, perhaps at annual intervals, with new ideas and standards being seen at each repetition.

The diagonal placement of apparatus is recommended, leaving space around each piece to enable floor work to be carried out.

The new balance principle involved in the work in part two is that the area of the base (given a similar body position) varies according to the surface upon which the body is supported, i.e. on an unrestricted surface, e.g. the floor, the area of the base is roughly represented by the rectangle a b c d.

On a restricted surface, e.g. a balance bar, the area of the base is represented by the rectangle w x y z.

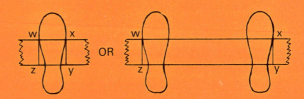

The size of base is therefore limited to the area in which friction is present between the weight-bearing part (in this case the feet) and the surface on which the weight is placed.

6.1

Locomotion

i   Locomotion involving the use of large shapes
ii Locomotion involving the use of small shapes
iii Locomotion involving both large and small shapes
iv Locomotion involving changing from large to small shapes and vice versa

N.B. These are movements where parts of the body are in contact with the floor at all times. There is no flight involved.

Similar work in series 5

Purpose

Revision of previous work. Emphasising the extremes of the range from full stretch to full curl.

Teaching points

Are you in the best shape for what you are doing?

Notes

An appreciation of suitability of shape for function (i.e. the best body shape for the movement) should be developed,

e.g. large and wide shape for cartwheeling movement or jumping,

small and round shape for forward and backward rolling movement.

6.2

Running and leaping showing first large stretching shapes in flight and later small tucked shapes

Similar work in series 4 and 5

Purpose

Extension of the experience of curling and stretching.

Teaching points

Remember that landings must be on two feet.

Position must be achieved quickly and changed again to prepare for a good safe landing, i.e. body must be stretched, and feet brought together before meeting the landing surface.

You will have to leap high to get a small tucked shape in flight.

Why is this?

Notes

The idea of opposite extremes of shapes (e.g. stretched or curled) will be familiar to the children. An understanding of possible intermediate stages should be developed, i.e. piked shapes, straddle shapes.

It should be made clear to the children that to vary shape in flight other than making a long stretch demands time to get into the shape and back to a stretch before landing.

6.3

Single floor movements involving different shapes using varying stages of size
See plate B (page 118)

Similar work in series 5

Purpose

To establish the concept of degrees of stretch or curl in movement.

Teaching points

Can you go from small to smaller to smallest?
Can you go from long to longer to longest?
Using also: *wide, tight.*

Notes

Movements and balances should be reasonably efficient and aesthetically pleasing.

Standards of quality and control must be maintained here.

Demonstrations and comparisons will help to establish an understanding of acceptable or unacceptable performance.

6.4

Single balances involving different shapes showing varying stages of size
e.g. small, smaller, smallest; wide, wider, widest

Similar work in series 5

Purpose

To establish the principle that balance is easier on a wide base than on a narrow base.

Teaching points

Can you show a long stretch, then a longer stretch, then the longest stretch you can possibly do?

Notes

Relationships between different shapes and their degree of stretch or curl should be emphasised.
(*This shape is larger than that.*)

6.5

Finding a balance position on a very small (or narrow) base e.g. on one point. Then finding a balance on a very large (or wide) base e.g. two points, widely spaced.

Similar work in series 2

Purpose

To establish the principle that balance is easier on a wide base than on a narrow base.

Teaching points

Which is easier – balancing on a small (narrow) base, or balancing on a large (wide) base?

Which position is a strong position?

If you are losing your balance when on a narrow base what can you do to recover?

Notes

We are attempting to promote the concept, in terms children can understand, that balance is only possible when the perpendicular line through the centre of gravity of the body falls within the area of the base, and therefore the larger or wider the area of the base, the easier it is to balance.

This can lead to very interesting and useful work in the classroom.

6.6

Movements and/or balances involving changing shapes and sizes

Similar work in series 5

Purpose

Further experience of balance principles acting upon children's own bodies.

Teaching points

Shape and size may be changed whilst holding a fixed base (points or patch).

Change your shape (or size) as you balance.

Notes

Example

Show a stretched balance on two points; change this to a curled balance on the same two points.

Use of words like **opposite** and **similar** can help vocabulary extension.

6.7

Joining two movements together which involve different or changing shapes (or sizes)

Purpose

Simple sequence building utilising the material learned.

Teaching points

Join two movements and balances in a wide shape. In your sequence show a change from a large to a small shape, or from a small to a large shape.

Notes

This extension may be developed to include other variables such as direction, speed, level, e.g. forward. backward, sideways, fast, slow, high level, low level.

series 6 part 2

Apparatus

As large a variety of pieces as possible. Similar pieces should be positioned to provide different situations, e.g. benches may be raised or inclined or inverted. A stool may be used by itself or with a bench or plank attached, etc.

6a

Movement of apparatus by groups

Similar work in all series

Notes

Emphasise the safety aspects of the positioning of apparatus.

6b

Exploration of movements on apparatus in specified shapes, i.e. wide, long, curled, etc.

Similar work in series 3 and 5

Purpose

Extension of concepts of use of body shape by using different levels, planes, surfaces.

Teaching points

Emphasis may be placed upon either movement or shape, i.e. *do the same movement in a wide/curled/long shape* or *find another way of moving on the apparatus in the same shape*.

Notes

One great difference between this and similar floor work is the use of different types of surfaces for support – not all are large and flat. The more variety which can be included, the more satisfactory the extension of the concept will be.

6c

Experimentation with balance on narrow or otherwise restricted surfaces, using both large and small bases

Similar work in series 2 and 5

Purpose
Wide and narrow bases of support used on restricted surfaces. Narrow base and narrow surface present the same difficulties, for the same reasons.

Teaching points
Can you balance on a small base (e.g. one point) on a small (narrow) surface (e.g. bench rib)?

Is it easier if you go on to two points?

Why is this?

Notes
Let the children experiment with this, freely and at length. The important concept in balance, at this stage, is that the smaller the base of support, the more difficult the balance, and vice versa. We want the children to understand this principle in terms of their own bodies and of the surface they are using.

6d

Exploration of balances and positions on apparatus, between two or more pieces or between apparatus and floor, or wall, in specified shapes

See plate C (page 119).

Similar work in series 5

Purpose
To widen children's balance experience, and to help them to grasp the concept that the base of support may be across different levels or different planes.

Teaching points
Balance on 3 points in a wide/curled/piked shape.

Find another balance on 3 points in the same shape.

Can you do it with your tummy looking up at the ceiling?

Can you do it with your tummy looking down at the floor?

Notes
Without being technical, the children should be helped to understand that a wide, and thus a stable base, need not be confined to a single surface. The strong position is a stable position.

6e

Building sequences involving different or changing shapes (or sizes) in both positions (balances) and movement

This may be done solely on apparatus or by using floor and apparatus.

Similar work in series 5

Purpose

An extension of all previous work on this theme.

Teaching points

Every attempt should be made to establish continuity in linking floor movements to apparatus movements and/or balances.

Notes

Having specified which shapes should be used in **6b,** you should allow free choice here. A variety of shapes should be used by each child.

6f

Replacement of apparatus

Similar work in all series

Notes

Give temporarily unoccupied children a task, e.g. any position which gives a strong feeling of balance.

This series pulls together the movement training that has been explored in individual areas in previous series. Initially it revises some of these, and then invites the children to put together sequences of balances and movements within fairly loose limitations. This enables every child to meet the requirements of the set task whilst working at his own level of achievement. In that it may fairly be assumed that at this point the individual skills of balances, different ways of moving and of landing will be reasonably well executed, the important new and creative element of linking these together is of paramount importance. Whilst realising that standards of good quality performance must be maintained throughout, the teacher should lay great stress on the linking movements, on the lines suggested in the **Notes** on the various activities.

The natural, and therefore normally the best way of moving out of a balance, is to move in the direction in which the body would topple if balance were lost, e.g. from a crouch balance or handstand. If balance is lost and the feet return to the floor to the same position they started from, the body-weight is moving backward, therefore the natural movement to follow is a backward movement – jump or roll.

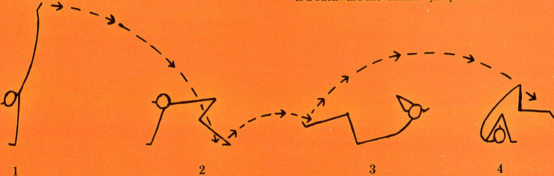

1   2   3   4

If balance is lost and the feet go beyond the balance position and would come to the floor ahead of hands, the body-weight is moving forwards, therefore the natural movement to follow is a forward movement – probably a roll.

The work in this series marks a breakthrough point in the child's movement experience. Having acquired various skills, and some understanding of the functions involved, he may now be asked to put the individual elements together in a creative and aesthetic sequence of movement.

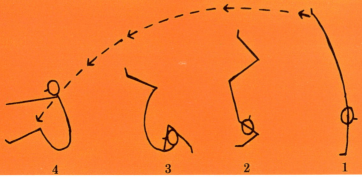

4   3   2   1

series 7 part 1

7.1

Travelling, using feet

Similar work in series 1, 2, 3, 4 and 5

Purpose

This whole series is a sideways development of previous work aimed at producing a better level of performance and a wider and more varied range of interpretation.

Teaching points

Having done this in previous themes, one can expect a variety of different ways of travelling on feet to be shown.

Differing directions, i.e. forwards, backwards, sideways, rotary or twirling. Differing speeds, i.e. fast or slow. Differing levels, i.e. high or low. Differing weights, i.e. heavy or light.

Notes

Maintenance of quality is very important – it can easily be lost here. The essential qualities are in **a** footwork **b** use of space **c** creative thinking – i.e. a variety of methods of moving. Foot remedial movements (**appendix 1**) may be used as part of this activity.

7.2

Travelling, using hands and feet

Similar work in series 3

Purpose

To enable a total rather than a partial weight transference to be practised and perfected.

Teaching points

The class might be encouraged to develop bunny jumps, catsprings, cartwheeling movements and, for the very able, walkovers. These, once achieved, should be promoted with changes of direction, speed, levels, etc.

Notes

See figs. 49, 53 and 54

In the feet and hands combination used at reception level it is mostly feet and hands used together in things like all-fours movement, whereas this transference requires the weight to be moved from the feet, on to the hands alone (even if only momentarily), and back to the feet.

7.3

Travelling on other body parts

Similar work in series 3

Purpose

To develop other means of weight transference.

Teaching points

A roll is a good (but not the only) way of moving from one position to another. See figs. 47, 48, 65 and 66.

When rolling, do not let your head touch the floor.

Notes

Many movements will come from this part of the theme. Not all of them will be aesthetically pleasing, creatively worthwhile and physically useful. Therefore avoid positions whose only merit is that they are different. Probably the most important element will be the rolls which children will perform. Once these have been established as a means of transferring weight from one part to another in order to travel, the various forms of roll should be taught (see **appendix 2**) in order to establish the correct principles and to minimise danger.

7.4

Balancing. Free work on different numbers and combinations of points and patches

Similar work in series 2

Purpose

Further development. Use of known principles of balance and extension of knowledge.

Teaching points

Balancing may be done on a varying number of points or patches or a combination of both. It can also be done with the body in various shapes, e.g. long and thin, or wide, or curled, etc.

It is harder on two points than on four – why?

It is harder on one foot than on two – why?

N.B. It will be even harder when they go on to apparatus – why?

It is not a balance until you can hold the position whilst you count silently 'one hundred, two hundred, three hundred'.

Can you find balance positions on two points other than standing?

If a part is supposed to be stretched, then stretch it – no bends at the knees or elbows.

Notes

It must also be noted by the teacher, and brought home to the children that, for example, not every three-point balance is easier than every two-point balance. A headstand, which is a three-point balance is harder than standing, which is a two-point. balance. Therefore the position in which a balance is attempted (e.g. upside down, sideways) affects ease or difficulty, and this is additional to the effects of the number of points or patches, size of base, etc.

These experiments with balance could be followed up in the classroom with simple experiments in principles of balance.

Stretching and curling cannot be themes in themselves, but they are theme developments which should be used extensively from this point onward. Ensure that stretches are really stretched and curls are really curled.

7.5

Sequences constructed from movements and positions already established

Similar work in series 5 and 6

Purpose

To utilise and develop skills already acquired by use in movement sequences. This will be a matter of combinations of various differing movements rather than repetitions of the same movements.

Teaching points

Can you move from a position (e.g. a three-point balance) to other positions, showing various ways of travelling?

The movement (method of travelling) should be attempted in different directions, and should also use different shapes of pathway (e.g. curve, zig-zag, L-shaped, etc.).

All the body of knowledge and experience of movement which has so far been accumulated should now be called upon and utilised. It is reasonable to expect to see some well finished work. The children and the teacher should also, by now, be speaking the same language with regard to the terms used in movement education.

All the teaching points which deal with neatness, control and continuity should now be used.

Notes

The work has now reached a point where children will be moving across bigger distances, and one must expect some children to move the length of the hall in order to express a sequence idea.

It may well be necessary to refer back to earlier training in use of space, since a number of children attempting large movement patterns at the same time in a small area could cause collisions or, probably worse, frustration when children are unable to complete planned sequences, because others are in the way.

Examples of the type of sequence that children might now be producing are:

a three-point balance, move to two-point balance, move to four-point balance; this might be performed as a headstand, roll forward to crouch balance, roll backward and into the crab position;

b balance on two hands and one foot, roll sideways and into balance on one hand and one foot, stand, leap high to finish in balance on all fours.

Apparatus

As many raised horizontal flat surfaces as possible (e.g. benches, boxes, movement table, supported planks, etc.). Suitable landing mats adjacent to pieces of apparatus

7a

Movement of apparatus by groups

Each group to be responsible for its own apparatus.

Similar work in all series

Teaching points

Ask the children to observe the positions in which apparatus is stored and ask them to tell you which apparatus should be moved first, and which last.

Notes

What you are asking the children to do, in terms of working out the order in which things should be moved, is valuable only if apparatus is always replaced in the same positions. This must be agreed by the entire staff, otherwise chaos will ensue. The more often a group of children moves the same apparatus, the more efficiently and quickly they will do it. Groups should be kept stable.

7b

Travelling, including negotiation of apparatus
Each group to use only its own apparatus

N.B. This is still a matter, as in part one, of travelling from point A to point B. The difference is that there is now a piece (or pieces) of apparatus to negotiate en route. In the case of climbing apparatus, the entire movement may take place on the apparatus.

In cases where there is only a small amount of apparatus available, floor work and apparatus work may be done at the same time (e.g. group 1 on floor, group 2 on apparatus) to avoid queuing for turns on apparatus. There should be as many groups as possible, in order to keep down the number of children in each group. Eight groups is a good division for the usual class at this level. Groups should change to a different piece of apparatus from time to time.

Purpose

To utilise and develop skills in a situation using apparatus, i.e. the children have travelled on the floor in part 1, they are now going to face the added challenge of doing the same type of travelling, negotiating apparatus whilst doing so.

Teaching points

Roll to the apparatus, pass over it using feet – hands – feet, then roll to finish the sequence.

Move to the apparatus using feet – hands – feet, show a balance on the apparatus and move away using feet – hands – feet.

Show a three-point balance then roll to the apparatus, pass over it using feet – hands – feet, etc.

There is an infinite variety of combinations of positions and movements based on work which has been done previously.

Notes

This enables the individual skills and sequences

which have been worked on the floor to be extended by introducing new dimensions, e.g. a cartwheel from a bench to the floor is really a different movement from the same cartwheel done on the floor because of the effects of gravity. This brings with it new problems which the child will solve with regard to flight, landing, etc.

N.B. At this stage, the child's level of physical ability is way above his level of understanding of function. Any explanations of the effects of gravity, should be limited to examples of those things which are obvious to the child, e.g. the higher the take-off point, the harder he hits the floor on landing.

7c

Replacement of apparatus by groups

Similar work in all series

Following on from the work done in **series 7,** this series continues with sequences and seeks to increase the quantity and quality of movements used.
The children should be encouraged to try movements which they can already perform.

Probably the most important considerations are

1   allowing the children plenty of time to practise
   a   individual balances and movements and
   b   complete sequences;
2   encouraging the children to produce a finished piece of work, i.e. from a starting position, through the sequence to a finishing position. Give the children frequent opportunities to see each

other's sequences, drawing attention to neat execution, flowing linking movements, ingenuity of sequence construction, etc.

It is advisable to institute a one-way system when the apparatus is in use, at least at the early stages, since children will be working from floor to apparatus and vice versa, and if direction of movement is entirely free, collisions might occur. The diagonal layout is again recommended. Following its initial use, this series should be used again from time to time, as children will produce new and different responses to the challenges as they acquire new individual skills and concepts.

8.1

Travelling, using feet

Similar work in series 1, 2, 3, 4, 5 and 7

Purpose

1 Return to basic work to reinforce concepts of good quality movement – e.g. lightness, control.
2 Formative work for feet and ankles.
3 To increase the variety of interpretation.

Teaching points

Bearing in mind the reasons for this, attempts should be made to place limitations upon the children's choice by asking for particular directions, speeds, levels, shapes, etc.

How many different ways can you move on your feet or on one foot?

Do not let your heels touch the floor.

Look into the space that you are going to move towards and make sure no one else is moving into it.

Notes

Foot remedial movements (**appendix 1**) may be used at this point. All space considerations still apply.

8.2

Weight transference – simple sequences

Similar work in series 7

Simple sequences, created by transferring weight from foot (feet) to foot (feet) and/or feet to hands to feet and/or feet to hands to another part and/or any part(s) to any part(s) and by using balances, as below, as starting, intermediate and finishing positions on one point, on two points, on three points, on four or more points, on patches.

A typical simple sequence might be: a balance on one point, moving into a feet-hands-feet movement, and finishing in a balance on four points.

Purpose

To raise the level of each child's skill and achievement, both in terms of movement and of creative thought.

Teaching points

There are a great many different (and desirable) ways of responding to the various challenges of feet-hands-feet or other body parts, etc. These can be drawn from the children by asking them to observe others, by simple suggestion or by suggesting a movement by a name which might be familiar to some of the children, e.g. cartwheel. The following positions and movements are within the potential ability of children of this age group, and might therefore be expected to be seen. If any of them do not appear, they might well be suggested to the children.

Travelling, feet-hands-feet
See figs. 61 to 64

a progressive bunny jumps

b cat spring, see **fig. 49**

c cartwheel, see **fig. 53**

d round-off (Arab wheel), see **fig. 62**

e   walkovers (particularly into and out of the crab position) see **figs. 54 and 64**

f   attempts at handwalking.

Travelling on other parts – which will be mainly in the form of rolls

a   forward rolls with variations to starting and finishing positions

b   backward rolls, with variations, see **figs. 65** and **66**

c   sideways rolling.

Children should be taught that the definition of balance is really intention to be stationary in a given position. They are aiming to be stationary for three seconds, but a momentary balance is acceptable.

Balancing
Balance with weight on hands

a   crouch balances

b   lifts from sitting or kneeling

c   high bunny jumps

d   handstand balance.

Other balances

In response to the challenge to show balances on any number of points or patches, children will produce a very wide variety of positions. Provided the position is reasonably functional the main consideration should be aesthetic and the teacher should therefore encourage balances which are aesthetically pleasing. The following positions are among those likely to be shown by children in response to various challenges.

a   Balances on one foot

b   Various types of headstand – as three-point balances

c   Crab position – as four-point balance

d   Balances in the sitting position as one-patch balances.

Notes
Understanding of function is very important. Children should be taught to feel the weight transference from, say, feet to hands and back to feet. This is a matter of, say, the hands bearing the weight of the body, rather than merely being in contact with the floor. Similarly, when kneeling, the knees are bearing the body-weight, although the toes may also be in contact with the floor.

Children must be taught to understand this.

It will be necessary to give time for the children to practise combining movements and/or balances. They should be given enough time to produce a finished sequence. To do this they will need to experiment to find suitable combinations.

Technical aspects of all these are described in **appendix 2**.

series
8 part **1**

Feet — hands — feet sequence

fig. 61

fig. 63

fig. 62

fig. 64

Backward roll

fig. 65

fig. 66

series 8 part 2

Apparatus

Benches, boxes, walking planks, vaulting pieces, movement tables and/or any other raised horizontal surfaces. Additionally, the means of raising or inclining benches, etc. e.g. trestles, stools, on climbing frames

8a

Movement of apparatus by groups

Similar work in all series

8b

Simple sequences based on the work in part one, using the apparatus as an additional challenge in negotiation. The floor should be used as well as the apparatus to obtain a variety of levels of working.

Similar work in series 7

Purpose

To utilise and develop skills in apparatus situations. To give further opportunities for children to observe and experiment with the effects of moving and balancing on restricted surfaces at various heights; of gravity on body-weight, etc.

Teaching points

It is intended that sequences should be developed making use of movements and balances (or positions) on both floor and apparatus. In addition to high quality movement, a wide range of variety in the content of the sequences should be sought.

This variety can be achieved as a result of variations in body parts bearing weight, types of movements, shapes, speeds and levels.

Additionally it can be obtained from variations in the way that apparatus can be negotiated, e.g. over, under, through, along, around, etc. (The use of these words should signify the many possibilities offered by each piece or complex of apparatus.)

Notes

The heights of apparatus should be graded to suit the ability levels of different groups.

Progression from previous work comes from the change in apparatus situations. Limitations imposed upon children can stimulate a wider range of movement, or can be used to concentrate practice of particular groups of skills.

New and additional words signifying new movements should be introduced during this work, such as climbing, swinging, suspended, supporting, hanging, circling.

The introduction of these words should assist in the communication required in the process of limitation suggested above.

Three-part sequences are probably long enough for this level, e.g. movement – balance – movement or balance – movement – balance.

8c

Landing

Landing on apparatus from a jump from the floor or another piece to start a sequence.

Landing on the mat after jumping or dropping from apparatus to finish the sequence.

Similar work in series 4

Purpose

Further practice in landing on various surfaces from various heights.

Teaching points

Important points involved in landings are

squashy

trunk upright

stretch to meet the floor.

Notes

For safety reasons revise earlier practice and emphasise care –

Be sure of a space for landing.

8d

Replacement of apparatus

Similar work in all series

This series seeks to extend the more natural jumping movements done previously to a point where formalised jumping techniques appropriate to various activities are mastered. Since the majority of the work is with apparatus, more sophisticated flight patterns and techniques may be explored. Additionally, since the effects of the force of gravity are increased by the height involved, landing techniques can be improved.

The body mechanics involved are closely allied to those affecting balance. Unfortunately, a landing which is aesthetically pleasing and physically safe is carried out with the legs and feet together, which provides a relatively small base. This makes control of the landing (which is really a sophisticated balance situation) more difficult than would be the case with a large base, i.e. feet apart.

Landings, however, must be made with the feet together, so the possibility of a large base is denied to the performer. Compensation for the small size of the base is provided by lowering the centre of gravity as the body gives at ankles, knees and hips (squashy), bringing the seat down almost to the heels. Mechanically, the nearer the centre of gravity to the base the more stable is the balance. If on landing, therefore, the centre of gravity can be kept immediately above the base and lowered as far as possible, control will be much easier to achieve. (See **figs. 51, 52** and **57**.)

Having made a squashy landing, children should be taught to stand erect without moving the feet. This shows that the landing has been controlled and puts a finish on the movement.

This control must be established before allowing children to progress to going direct from landing into another movement, e.g. **9e**.

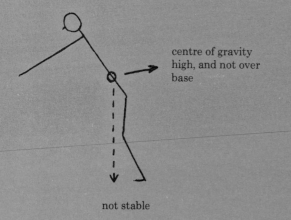

centre of gravity high, and not over base

not stable

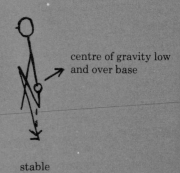

centre of gravity low and over base

stable

9.1

**Running, with high jumps, to land to stop.
(Single-foot take-off, double-foot landing)**

Similar work in series 4

Purpose

To teach single-foot take-off whilst running.

Teaching points

The standing position after the landing should be
held as a balance for 3 seconds to demonstrate
control before running on.

Squashy landing.

Keep hands off the floor when landing,
Keep the trunk upright as you land,
Do not let the heels touch the floor.

Notes

See fig. 67

The running, single-foot take-off leap is one of the
most useful skills a child can learn. Its application in
play, formal games, athletics, etc., is almost
boundless. Some children find the co-ordination
difficult. If previous series dealing with basic weight
transference have not been covered, it can be taught
as foot – foot – foot – feet.

fig. 67

9.2

**Running, with high jumps, showing stretched
position in flight**

Similar work in series 4 and 5

Purpose

Control of flight in the most manageable body
position.

Notes

See figs. 68 and 69

Do not ask for variations of flight position at this
point as it is unlikely children will leap high enough
to have time to get into and out of any other flight
position. It may be helpful to place large hoops on the
floor and encourage children to land in the hoop
without teetering out of it.

fig. 68

series 9 part 2

Apparatus
Raised flat surfaces, e.g. benches, top section of vaulting box, walking planks, movement table, etc. Landing mats

9a

Movement of apparatus by groups

Similar work in all series

Teaching points
Best placement of apparatus with view to **a** safety **b** room to work.

Notes
Wherever possible have the landing side of apparatus towards the centre of the hall. It is dangerous to have children landing in the direction of a wall or any other obstruction.

fig. 69

9b

Leaping from raised surface to land to stop (flight off)

Similar work in series 4

Purpose
Revision of landing technique and further practice.

Teaching points
Different positions in flight, stretched, curled, wide. It is important to get into a stretched position before landing.
Can you jump from one/two feet?
Can you still land to stop?
Keep trunk upright when landing.

Notes
See figs. 51 and 52

Children will tend to do a double-foot take-off from apparatus. This is not important, provided they appreciate the difference.

Leaps should be for height rather than length.

All flight positions must return to the stretch before landing.

See **figs. 72** and **73** and note the balance in flight, the body beginning to stretch to meet the landing, and the intense concentration.

9c

Leap from raised surface to land and roll forward

Once the roll is achieved safely and well, other forward movements may be substituted, e.g. bunny jump, a second leap, etc.

Purpose

Control of landing and addition of a movement to follow.

Teaching points

Much more weight has to be taken on the hands at the beginning of the roll than was necessary from a stationary start.

When you land from the leap, your movement is carrying you forward.

That is why you carry on with another movement – the roll.

Make sure your head doesn't touch the mat.

Notes

It may be better to ask for a curl, followed by a stretch in flight, rather than just a curl. Do not ask for twists (turns) in flight at this point.

A reference back to (and perhaps further practice on) previous work might well be worthwhile, or even necessary, at this point.

A stretched (long) flight position, being easiest, is best to start with.

When children are managing to control the landing and roll, different positions may be used. This activity may be extended indefinitely by adding more floor work to follow the roll, e.g. flight off – land – roll – balance – roll – stand.

9d

Leap from floor to land on apparatus

Single-foot take-off (flight on), flight off as in **9b** and **9c**.

Similar work in series 4

Purpose

Landing on a restricted surface – this is both landing and balance.

Teaching points

If this is done slowly, it is easy. If it is done fast, it is difficult.

Why is this?

(Because feet and legs stop, but the top part of the body wants to keep going.)

How can we make it easier?

(Land in the deepest possible crouch, this lowers the centre of gravity making balance easier, or extend the arms sideways to achieve the same effect.)

Deep squash to land, stand up and leap high.

Notes

See figs. 70 and 76

This should first be done from a standing position, but as soon as children are able, it should be done from running. The most important part of this activity is the first landing on the apparatus, so do not permit any on-off movements. The movement sequence, at this moment, should be on-pause-stand-off. There is another possible mathematical link here, since the centre of gravity is under consideration.

The following is a development of **9d** which children may discover for themselves. Whilst it is not suggested that this is necessarily the next activity, the following points should be observed, should they arise.

Leap from raised surface, half turn in flight, to land, to stop. Once established a backward movement may be added after the landing, as in **9c**.

Purpose

To establish change of direction in flight.

Teaching points

Double-foot landing. A long, thin, stretched position in flight makes the half-turn easier.

When you land, your movement is carrying you backward. If you add another movement it should be a backward movement.

Notes

See fig 71

In early attempts keep the leap fairly low. With a half-turn the child will land facing the apparatus from which he has leapt.

9e

Running to apparatus. Single-foot take-off to single-foot landing on apparatus immediately followed by take-off to double-foot landing (flight on and off)

Once established, variations and additional movements may be added, as in **9c** and **9d**.

Purpose

Controlled flight on and second take-off. This is an activity which will have many uses at a later stage.

Teaching points

Run over the top.

Notes

Some children may wish to make the movement on and the movement off into separate movements. This is natural, but what we are after is on-off as a continuous movement.

Benches are suitable for this activity.

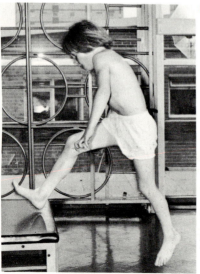

fig. 70

fig. 71

9f

Running, single-foot take-off leap over apparatus (flight over)

This can be a double-foot landing to stop, or into another movement. It can be to a single-foot landing (hurdling action) to run on or to stop.

Purpose
Formalisation of jumping techniques.

Teaching points
This can be done as a long-jump type leap – single-foot take-off to double-foot landing to stop. It may be performed as a hop or a scissor-jump, single-foot take-off to single-foot landing to stop. These are basic high jump techniques. It may be performed hurdling style by striding over – single-foot take-off to single-(other) foot landing to continue running.

Notes
Canes across skittles may be introduced to supplement benches, etc.

9g

Replacement of apparatus

Similar work in all series

fig. 72

fig. 73

This series seeks to achieve two things;

1 an extension of the children's range of skills in floor movement, which will enable further creative work to be done,

2 the ability to pass over apparatus, initially with the weight on the hands, which can be loosely described as vaulting.

It is important to be aware that there is nothing undesirable in children learning skills which are described as formal, e.g. movements such as handsprings, through and astride vaults, provided that there is no insistence that every child attempts that particular movement. Neither is there anything particularly desirable in encouraging children to persevere with movements that are lacking in either functional or aesthetic value, but whose only virtue is that of being different.

Basically, what is inherent in the work is to establish sound, efficient and safe techniques for approaching vaulting type activities. This means the mastery of the technique of the running, double-footed take-off. It is this take-off which, in almost all activities of this kind, ensures a balanced, and therefore safe, flight, either on to, off or over the apparatus. It is only from a balanced flight that a balanced landing is likely to result.

10.1

Moving at different speeds and transferring weight to and from different body parts whilst maintaining movement

Similar work in series 3

Purpose

To obtain a variety of connected movements which flow one into another.

Teaching points

Flow does not necessarily mean constant speed. Sometimes the quality of the flow of movement might not be smooth. It may be one of stops and starts. This is acceptable, provided it is intentional, in that the movements selected demand it.

Can you make a change of direction as you move?

Can you do a series of movements which keeps you low/high?

Can you move backwards/sideways during your sequence?

Notes

The sort of thing that is looked for is,
run – leap – land – roll – stand – run,
cartwheel (or other feet – hands – feet movement) –
leap – run – roll – leap – half turn – roll – run.
It is beneficial to refer to the various movements (to the children) by both the name of the movement, e.g. bunny jump, cartwheel; and its description in terms of body parts used, e.g. feet – hands – feet.

10.2

Travelling, feet – hands – feet

Similar work in series 3 and 7

Purpose

Raising level of performance in basic movement pattern. Extending children's range of responses to this pattern.

Teaching points

Children should be encouraged to try to **a** improve the quality of the movement they are doing, and **b** attempt new movements, e.g. a bunny jump may be improved to become a cat spring by having a short period of flight between take-off and landing. A cartwheel may become an Arab wheel by bringing the legs together when in the vertical upside-down position.

Notes

A higher standard of performance is to be expected than was obtained at **series 7** stage. This will manifest itself in such things as limbs that are intended to be stretched are really stretched, e.g. legs straight, toes pointed; overall control of the movement shown by lightness of landing.

fig. 74

10.3

Running, to leap from a double-foot take-off

Purpose

To teach double-foot take-off technique in a safe situation, i.e. on the floor.

Teaching points

In movement terms this is foot – foot, etc., foot – feet – feet, or *one, one, one,* etc., *one, two, two.*

In essence, this is a little one-to-two jump followed by a high two-to-two jump.

Demonstration is of great assistance in this movement.

Make your landings squashy.

Stretch to meet the floor.

Notes

See fig. 74

This double-foot take-off is essential for safety in most vaulting type movements, from a simple leap frog to more sophisticated feet – hands – feet movements across or over apparatus. This is not an easy skill for many children, and much practice and many demonstrations by children who can do it may well be necessary. To see a child attempt, say, a simple leap frog movement from a single-foot take-off will show the danger in allowing children to proceed to this type of activity before mastering a double-foot take-off.

10.4

Running forward movements from double-foot take-off (rolls, leaps etc.)

N.B. Rolls to be performed on landing mats

Purpose

Use of double-foot as take-off for another movement.

Teaching points

It is most important that the head makes no contact with the floor in the roll. Take it very slowly on the first attempts. The take-off flows into the movement. *Lift your bottom as you take off for the roll.*

Notes

Let children do this slowly until a pattern is established. Indeed, there is no virtue in the run-up being fast. It is an attempt to establish and **groove** a rather difficult pattern of movement. Leaps and rolls are suggested since these are **a** within the compass of children's ability at this stage, and **b** attempts at other movements initiated on the move (e.g. bunny jump) will have disastrous consequences for some children. By all means let children be creative in selecting their movements, but be sure the initial attempts are performed very slowly, so that children can discover the feeling of the movements when done on the move and work out whether or not the movements are safe when performed at greater speed.

10.5

In threes: leap frog over a partner's back
See fig. 75

Purpose

Flight over with feet – hands – feet weight
transference.

Teaching points

Making of back is very important. Must be firmly
based and reasonably rigid.

Take off from two feet.

Big jump.

Try to keep your trunk upright in flight.

Deep squashy landing to stop.

Notes

To make the back, stand with one foot forward with
both hands on forward leg just above the knee. Chin
on chest to keep head out of the way.

For safety, make sure that a double-foot take-off
is used.

fig. 75

Apparatus

Apparatus with horizontal surfaces at varying heights, e.g. benches, movement tables, vaulting boxes or box tops, flat top trestles, etc., landing mats

10a

Movement of apparatus
Similar work in all series

The following is a selection of activities involving a feet – hands – feet weight transference from a double-foot take-off. These may be teacher-directed or they may arise from the children's own exploration of the floor work principles applied on apparatus. However they are arrived at, the following activities may be useful. For methods of support, see **appendix 3.**

fig. 76

10b(i)

Double-foot take-off to hands – feet transfer, to land on apparatus (fig. 76)
High leap off, to land

Purpose

Development of floor work.

Teaching points

To land on apparatus
a with feet between hands
b with feet outside hands
c with both feet beside hands (feet together)
d any other appropriate movements the children might attempt.

Having got on the apparatus, the children might well be encouraged to experiment with feet – hands – feet (or any other weight transferring movement) along the apparatus before leaping off. This may be done either by going on at the end and moving along, or by going on at the side and changing direction to move along. This is, in fact, apparatus sequence work.

Notes

This activity can be described as vaulting on to apparatus in various ways. Apparatus which is too low, e.g. a bench, creates more problems than it solves. Ideal apparatus height is about waist high to the children. At this point, use of horizontal bars on climbing frames to suspend such things as benches, etc., become very useful. Some children, on account of nervousness, lack of ability, etc., will transfer feet – hands – knees rather than feet – hands – feet. This should be accepted, and children should be encouraged to try to land on feet, by lifting the bottom at take-off. At this stage, where vault-type activities are being undertaken, there is nothing wrong, *per se,* with the use of beating boards. These merely raise the level of the floor, thus lowering the effective height of the apparatus, and this is desirable for some children.

10b(ii)

Running forward, double-foot take-off to hands – feet transfer to go over apparatus

Purpose

Development of basic vaulting techniques.

Teaching points

Various ways of negotiating the apparatus are
a one leg on each side (straddle vault) **fig. 77**
b both legs to same side (side vault)
c both legs between arms (squat vault) **fig. 78.**
Feet may pass the sides of the apparatus or over the top. See also **figs. 79** and **80.**

Keep head up.

No matter how you go over, try to stretch to meet the floor as you land.

Notes

Here again, for safety reasons, stress the importance of taking-off from two feet. Stress squashy landings.

fig. 77

10b(iii)

Running forward, double-foot take-off to other movements initiated from weight on hands

e.g. rolls on apparatus, i.e. the hands must be the first part of the body to touch the apparatus.

Purpose

Further development of vaulting and other skills on apparatus.

Teaching points

Additional ways of getting on to or over apparatus following a run.

Get plenty of spring and lift your bottom at take-off for a roll.

Notes

Initially, this should only be attempted where the surface of the apparatus is long enough to accommodate the roll and should ideally have a padded surface. See **fig. 81.**

The hands should be placed flat on top of the apparatus, not gripping the sides.

Other possibilities arising are cartwheel along the apparatus (**fig. 80**), handstand on the apparatus with a quarter twist-off both from a double-foot take-off.

fig. 78

series **part**

10 2

10c

Replacement of apparatus

Similar work in all series

fig. 80

fig. 81

fig. 79

This series seeks to exploit the skills acquired or improved previously by asking the children to use them in a creative situation. At this point merely to talk of creative work can be a sterile exercise. To make the situation purposefully creative, the children must be observed carefully, and guided. If one draws an analogy between a sequence of movement and a piece of music, the same basic considerations apply. In the same way that music is not created by the repetition of a single note, a movement sequence is not created by continually using the same movement. A piece of music has a definite starting point, it has contrast between one part and another, it has high points and low points, it probably has a climax and a definite finishing point. A movement sequence should have much the same qualities and, equally important, it should give satisfaction to both its creator – the child, and the observers – other children and the teacher. At this stage, one does not expect the child to create a full symphony, but it is not unreasonable to expect a pleasant tune, in terms of the musical analogy.

Allow the children plenty of time to work out, to practise and to perfect sequences. As has been said several times previously, the greater the range of skills the child possesses, the greater is his creative potential. He has the tools with which to tackle the task. It often happens that in attempting to create a sequence, a child is inhibited by his inability to perform what he sees as the right movement at a given point. In such cases a fertile teaching and learning situation exists, and teachers might well make great progress in teaching individual movements in lessons which are ostensibly devoted to sequence work.

11.1

i **Moving on feet**
ii **Moving, feet – hands – feet**

Similar work in series 1, 2, 3, 4, 5, 7 and 8

Purpose

Revision of previous work. Maintenance and improvement of quality of movement. Preparation for sequence.

Teaching points

Ask especially for high jumps and good quality landings.

Encourage feet – hands – feet movements which cause the children to travel over large distances, e.g. cartwheel rather than bunny hop.

Notes

Children should be encouraged to use the whole range of movements they have acquired through previous work, plus any others they might discover.

11.2

Balance position, linked to a second balance by a movement

Later a balance position, linked to a second balance by a series of movements.

Similar work in series 2, 5, 7 and 8

Purpose

Controlled movement, i.e. ability to stop and balance. Encouragement of natural flows, e.g. speed, direction, level, of movement.

Teaching points

It is easier to go into a balance from a slow movement than from a fast one.

The natural direction to go from a balance is the way you would go if you lost your balance and toppled over.

Hold each balance for three seconds.

If your second balance is, for example, a single-point balance, can you arrive in this position rather than finish your movement on two points and then change to one?

Notes

Start from a balance – to (single) movement – to balance situation. This will enable children to grasp the concepts of

1 a controlled flow of speed and rhythm out of and into a balance
2 the natural direction and level of movement from and to a balance.

N.B. The natural movement out of and into a static position is invariably the most pleasing from the aesthetic viewpoint.

Examples

a **Very simple**

One-point balance – movement to a different one-point balance, e.g. single-foot balance, followed by single-foot leap to single-foot balance on other foot.

b Slightly more difficult

Three-point balance – movement to patch balance, e.g. balance on one foot and two hands, followed by roll forward to seat balance (with hands and feet off floor).

c More difficult

Three-point balance – movement to two-point balance, e.g. headstand followed by knee and elbow hand balance. (**fig. 14**)

d Backward sequence

Two-point balance − movement to one-point balance, e.g. knee and elbow hand balance followed by roll backward to single-foot balance.

e Sideways sequence

One-point balance − movement to different one-point balance, e.g. single-foot balance followed by cartwheel to single-foot balance on other foot.

It is now reasonable to ask for a definite, and permanently agreed starting and finishing position to be adopted at the start and finish of each sequence, be it short or long. The standing position (feet together, hands at sides) is recommended.

This tends to put polish and finish on the work.

11.3

Extension and development of 11.2 by increasing the number of either balances or linking movements or both

Teaching points

This can be further developed by using variations of speed, direction, level and strength (or weight) of movement. The teacher can help greatly by watching individuals, prompting, suggesting and questioning them about their work.

Should these toes be pointed?

How can you improve the link between these two movements?

You may be able to twist as you roll to help you change direction.

Notes

Sequences: these should be developed as finished pieces of work. After opportunities have been given to experiment, select and practise the parts of the sequence. Emphasis should be placed on continuity, flow and control. The order and contents should then become established. Much use should be made of observation by children of each other's work to develop a critical eye and an understanding of good form.

Apparatus

Maximum possible, plus landing mats

11a

Movement of apparatus

Similar work in all series.

11b

Floor sequence, as in 11.3 but negotiating a single piece of apparatus at some time during the sequence

At first, give each group a set piece of apparatus around which to work. Choice comes later.

Purpose

Inclusion of apparatus in the sequence as a further progression.

Teaching points

You can go over, under, through, etc. when you come to the apparatus.

You can change direction as you negotiate the apparatus.

We need a single movement to negotiate the apparatus, e.g.
on – off or over.

If we get little sequences on the apparatus everyone else will have to wait.

Notes

The manner in which the apparatus is negotiated should, at first, be left to the children. Until they become accustomed to the idea do not encourage static positions, e.g. balances, on the apparatus, since this causes a bottleneck for the rest of the group.

The quality, finish, etc. must not be allowed to deteriorate, at this point. Introduction of apparatus tends to cause this. Give the same opportunities for practice and exploration as in part one but once sequences become established, do not accept any deterioration in the quality of movement. Give each group plenty of time on one piece of apparatus – the whole of part two of a lesson might not be too long.

11c

As 11b, but having each group negotiating two pieces of apparatus, or using the same piece twice in the sequence

This might be worked, if apparatus is available, by giving each group a small apparatus complex.

Notes

If a group is using the same apparatus twice in a sequence, the teacher may have to impose a directional traffic system to avoid collisions. Properly organised, this will keep the children on the move, but it can cause queuing if the teacher is not careful.

11d

Extension of 11b and 11c to include free movement on floor and any apparatus (but preferably not all apparatus)

Notes

This is the ultimate in free movement at this stage. It is also the ultimate in confusion potential if the children have not been carefully guided toward it via **11b** and **11c.** It may be that an intermediate step – e.g. each child working half the hall (and thus half the apparatus) – may be worthwhile.

11e

Replacement of apparatus

Similar work in all series

This theme is an extension of work already covered on an individual basis. Having worked out and performed combinations and sequences of movement, the child is now asked to combine with another to produce similar work, as a duet. This seems to have values beyond the purely physical and creative, in that the child is put in a position whereby he has to consider the strengths and weaknesses of someone else before deciding what is to be done, and perhaps modify his own desires, accordingly.

On the basic level, at the start of the series, the work is no more than an exercise in mutual timing, but as the theme progresses other considerations arise. For instance, the child must consider his partner's ability to perform certain movements and combinations; he must consider what length of time each requires to perform a given movement; he must observe how far both travel in performing the same movement, before what the pair is going to do is decided. The same applies to the manner of performance.

These partner activities can be infinitely extended by varying what is actually done, and by varying the conditions under which it is done, e.g. shadow, or mirror, or variations of either or both of them.

A relatively free placement of apparatus will have to be organised for part two of the lessons, since the type of apparatus used and its placement will depend upon the type of work that is being done.

12.1

Any form of moving, on feet, in pairs, attempting to keep together and move in time with each other

Purpose

First concepts of shadow partner work.

Teaching points

It is easier to do this when movement is slow, e.g. walking rather than running.

Watch your partner and 'feel' his movements.

Notes

It will probably be necessary to revert to the circle around the hall for this. Whilst reminding the class to **remain 'space aware'**, it should be realised that most of their concentration will go toward the timing and adjustment of movement. This activity should be worked through many forms of moving on feet; walking, running, hopping, jumping, to ensure plenty of practice.

For much of part one, individual mats, or something similar, are desirable since it is wise to limit the range of movement which pairs of children are to attempt to co-ordinate. The mat is a convenient small area around which to work. This is probably necessary because it is unlikely that children will yet understand the more refined special concepts which apply to partner work. Later, large landing mats might be necessary for some pairs.

12.2

In pairs, any movement across the mat (or space) performed side by side, in time

Purpose

Practice in moving in time with a partner.

Teaching points

Co-operation, e.g. each partner being willing to adjust his movement to fit another's is absolutely necessary.

This presents an opportunity to test his ability to do so.

Watch your partner and 'feel' his movements.

One of the pair start the movement by saying 'one-two-three – go' or something similar.

This is called shadow work because it is like watching a person and his shadow.

Notes

See figs. 82, 83 and 84.

Initially the priorities are

1 mutual timing

2 sophistication of movement.

It follows that children might well be advised to keep the movement itself quite simple at this stage in order to get the timing right.

fig. 82

fig. 83

fig. 84

12.3

As 12.2 but starting from opposite sides of the mat, or space

Purpose

Development of timing techniques.

Teaching points

Keep your movement slow and simple until you are working well in time together.

Try to start far enough apart so that you can see each other all the time.

This way you will make sure you finish side by side.

Notes

This is not strictly shadow, but it is a useful method of reinforcing the concept of small group combined or co-operative movement. The advantage of this is that the two children can easily see each other for most of the time. (See **fig. 85**)

fig. 85

12.4

In pairs, side by side, working across the mat, or space. Balance position on n points, followed by a movement

Purpose

Extending the shadow concept by adding to the task.

Teaching points

This is more difficult, since the timing has now to take into account

a the duration of the held balance

b the movement itself.

Time it by counting. See **12.2**

Can you do it by counting silently?

Notes

This is an extension of **12.2**, increasing the difficulty of the timing. Children should be given plenty of time for free practice and experiment, during which time the teacher should be occupied helping, suggesting and supporting, where necessary.

fig. 86

12.5

Further extensions of 12.4, e.g.

i   balance – movement – balance

ii movement – movement – balance, etc.

Purpose

Further extension of the shadow concept.

Teaching points

Timing becomes even more difficult as the number of movements, etc. increases. Even more individual adjustments become necessary.

Notes

Ensure that mats are available to pairs who are using movements where a mat is desirable.

Equally, for some sequences, mats are positively undesirable. This especially applies to jumping movements.

12.6

**Directional extensions of 12.4 and 12.5,
e.g. movement – balance – movement, showing a
change of direction**

Purpose

Further extension of the shadow concept.

Notes

In this series each progression is considerably more
difficult than the last. Give children plenty of
opportunity for practice, and perfect each activity
before moving on. Some pairs, no doubt, will be
ready to move on before others.

12.7

**Extension of 12.4, 12.5 and 12.6 by use of various
levels**

e.g. variation of level of a starting position – high,
low, etc., starting the sequence on a high level and
finishing on a low level, starting low, going to high
and finishing low, etc.

Purpose

Extension of the shadow concept by using varying
levels.

This can now be even further extended by asking for
variations of speed, of lightness and strength of
movement, of smooth or jerky flow, etc. The
permutations of the four qualities of time, weight,
space and flow are numerous.

It can be even further extended by repeating the
whole of part one with the children working mirror
instead of shadow. This entails one partner acting as
the other's reflection, as in a mirror. See below.

Shadow

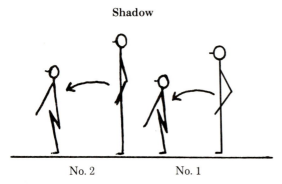

No. 2   No. 1

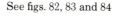

See figs. 82, 83 and 84

Mirror

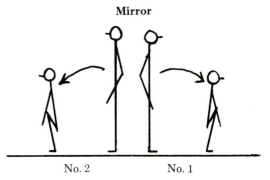

No. 2   No. 1

See fig. 86

Apparatus

Any apparatus large enough for two children to work on at the same time

Landing and individual mats

12a

Movement of apparatus

Similar work in all series

Notes

Leave adequate space between apparatus for floor work to be done.

12b

In pairs, synchronised movement, on, off and over the apparatus

Purpose

Extension of floor work.

Teaching points

Such considerations as speed of run-up, length of take-off and landing flight now become important, and further mutual adjustment is necessary.

Notes

All the principles which apply in part one still apply. As you have introduced a new dimension in the form of apparatus, simple activities are indicated at the start of part two. Again, plenty of practice is needed and do not be in too much of a hurry to move on.

12c

In pairs, floor movement to apparatus; on, off and over apparatus to landing; floor movement away from apparatus

Purpose

Combination, floor and apparatus, in shadow.

Notes

This is sophisticated work and needs to be approached slowly and carefully. It should be built up by starting with a floor movement with which the pair is familiar from part one. To this should then be added the apparatus movement that the pair used in the last activity, **12b.** Only when these have been perfected as an integrated whole should the final floor movement be added.

12d

Extension of 12c

The work done in **12c** can now be extended indefinitely, using the time, weight, space and flow variations as shown in the **Notes** in part one. Now apparatus is involved, additionally to floor work, the possibilities become infinite.

Notes

Such challenges as *show me a sequence which starts at a low level, shows weight on hands at some point and passes over the apparatus, finishing at a medium level,* should now be used.

It is to be hoped that by now the children will have both skill and understanding, and therefore to ask for different methods of performance now has some point, and should be productive of good creative work.

N.B. All the work in this series may be duplicated in mirror principles. This is a considerable progression from shadow work and much more difficult for the children, so it should be introduced gradually, and very simply, perhaps single challenges in mirror as in extension of any shadow activity.

12e

Replacement of apparatus

Similar work in all series

In this series, a new concept is introduced, that of one partner bearing the other's body-weight in different ways. The first consideration, as always, must be for the children's safety, and the teacher should therefore take care that the class is led progressively into the more difficult situations by ensuring that the earlier activities in the series are done properly, and that the children understand the principles involved. For this work *make haste slowly* should be the guiding principle for the teacher.

The more adventurous members of the class will want to proceed, eventually, to some frightening looking exercises, e.g. one partner standing on the other's shoulders. There is no reason why they should not be permitted to do so provided that

a they can do so on suitable matting, i.e. agility or safety mattress

b they have proved their ability to perform such a balance at lower levels, e.g. with the weight bearer sitting on the floor or in a kneeling position

c they have discussed and practised the loss of balance escape route, which is usually done by the balancer jumping forward – downward

d there is a catcher, or catchers, standing by to assist, if necessary.

This is very much a case of striking an acceptable balance between, on the one hand, limiting children's achievements because of a teacher's timidity, and on the other, protecting children from their own rashness and lack of a proper sense of judgement.

This work can produce some most delightful results, even with the less physically able children, particularly if, when the fundamentals of partner weight-bearing have been established, it is linked with work from the previous series. The result is one of children doing matched sequences leading up to a two child (or more) tableau situation. This, in one activity, seems to fulfil most of the objectives of physical education, in that to perform it successfully, strength and skill must be used: each partner must

have a total consideration for his partner's ability, or lack of it, and for his safety and comfort: there must be an aesthetic appreciation of what they are doing, the child is gaining self-realisation through his and his partner's creative ability: physical and mechanical problems must be recognised and solutions sought: and since the whole thing consists of skills which the child recognises as worthy, it is socially acceptable and satisfying to him. Again a free placement of apparatus should be used, according to the nature of what the children are attempting.

N.B. Throughout this series, partners should be matched by weight.

13.1

Individual balance work on 1, 2 or 3 points

Similar work in series 2 and 7

Purpose

Revision of balance principles.

Teaching points

Try variations of position, i.e. the same basic position with

a body looking at the floor

b body looking at the ceiling

c body looking at the wall.

Notes

This series could, if allowed, become static. Break up the lesson pattern by asking for moving activities between balances.

fig. 87

13.2

Matching balances

i.e. both partners balancing on same body parts and using same body shape. May be done independently, but attempts should be made for balances to be synchronised, i.e. shadow movement into and out of the balance

Similar work in series 12

Purpose

a Adaptation of own performance to meet the demands of combined activities.

b To help create a clearer understanding of functional and aesthetic requirements of balances and movements used.

c To help concentration on details of partner's performances.

Teaching points

Variety of ways of carrying out each activity.

You must watch your partner carefully in order to copy accurately.

Notes

See figs. 87 and 88

A fairly high degree of freedom of choice must be given in order that children can make use of their most skilful movements and balances. Standards of control and quality should be insisted upon in these partner work developments of previously taught activities.

13.3

Linked balances

In pairs, balance position on 4 points between the two partners. Later vary number of points and/or patches.

Purpose

Co-operation and discovery of principles involved in mutual weight-bearing.

To develop confidence in the partner's ability to help.

Teaching points

If you are going to support all, or any part, of your partner's weight, you must know what he is going to do.

If you are the partner who is going to take the weight, you must make a strong position for yourself.

What is the strongest position you know?
(Normally a leap frog back, or on all fours.)

What are other strong positions?
(Standing with feet apart.)

What makes a position strong?
(Wide, stable base with weight evenly distributed across the base. Firm surface on which to take the position.)

Notes

See figs. 89 – 93

In this activity, partners will have some physical link with each other. Thus, various combinations of the number of points each has in contact with the floor are possible, e.g.

$4 + 0 = 4$

Example: One partner in a face downward bridge position, with hands and feet on floor; other partner sitting astride his back, with no parts contacting the floor.

$3 + 1 = 4$

Example: One partner in headstand, with forehead and hands in contact with floor; other partner in single-foot balance position, supporting first partner's legs with one hand.

$2 + 2 = 4$

Example: One partner, standing with two feet in contact with floor, supports other partner with two hands in contact with floor in a wheelbarrow position.

fig. 88 ·

fig. 89

fig. 91

fig. 90

fig. 92

13.4

In pairs, linked balance on points and/or patches, move to matching balance

Purpose

More advanced application of principles in **12.2** and **12.3**.

Teaching points

The first thing to decide is how you are going to move out of your linked balance in a way which is safe for both of you.

Notes

Because the partners will start from different positions, the movements which link the two balances will be different. Children should start by moving out of the linked balance. Having done so, they might be in almost any position, standing, sitting or lying. It is from this position that they should move to the matching balance.

fig. 93

13.5

In pairs, linked balance, where one partner bears the other's weight

Purpose

Further experience of bearing weight, and having weight borne.

Partner co-operation and confidence.

Teaching points

To take your partner's weight, you need a really strong position.

This starts with a firm strong base.

If you are going to put your weight on your partner, be sure you put it on a strong part.

Notes

See figs. 94 – 100

This activity should be initiated at a low level, e.g. one partner on all fours, the other sitting astride his shoulders or lower back. This is done to establish the ability of one partner to bear the whole of the other's weight, and to give children the opportunity to practise these balances in safety and with confidence, before going on to more difficult work.

fig. 94

fig. 95

fig. 96

fig. 97

fig. 98

fig. 99

fig. 100

Note the concentration of the catchers

13.6

In pairs, linked balance where partners balance each other by opposition of weight

Purpose

Bearing weight in opposition.

Teaching points

Which is the best way of supporting each other with your weights in opposition?

Notes

See figs. 101 – 104

The simplest form of this activity is for the two partners to stand close together back to back and lean against each other. It can be developed by joining hands when facing each other and leaning back against each other's weight, and by standing side by side, joining hands and leaning outward. Variations of these are possible by moving other limbs to new positions. This work is static and should be carried out for short periods only.

fig. 101

series **13** **part** **1**   Linked balances

fig. 102

fig. 104

fig. 103

Apparatus

All available pieces on which children can position themselves. Raised horizontal surfaces and climbing frames are especially suitable. Landing mats.

13a

Movement of apparatus

Similar work in all series

13b

Partners supporting each other's weight by opposition

Purpose

Extension of weight-bearing concepts.

Notes

This is the logical progression from **13.6**. The possibilities are limited when working on the floor. On apparatus they are very considerably increased. Where fixed horizontal bars (as on climbing frames) are available, the work may be further extended by use of strong skipping ropes as cantilevers, with partners holding the ends.

This, like **13.6**, is static in nature, and should be undertaken for short periods only, rather than for a whole lesson.

13c

Replacement of apparatus

Similar work in all series

The work in this series introduces a new concept.
This may well link with work in mathematics. If this
is done, or has been done, explanations in P.E.
lessons will probably be at a minimal level, since
the children will be able to apply their knowledge of
symmetry and asymmetry to body positions and
movements.

Some children might find difficulty in grasping the
concept of symmetry when working with a partner.
In such cases, work in the classroom with an ink blot
or paint on a piece of paper which is then folded, will
help them to grasp the concept of two asymmetrical
halves producing a symmetrical whole, e.g.

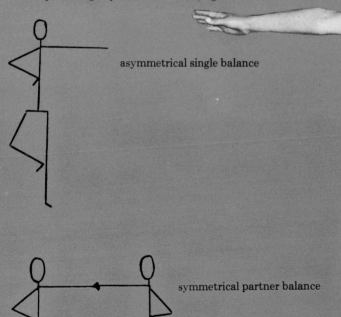

asymmetrical single balance

symmetrical partner balance

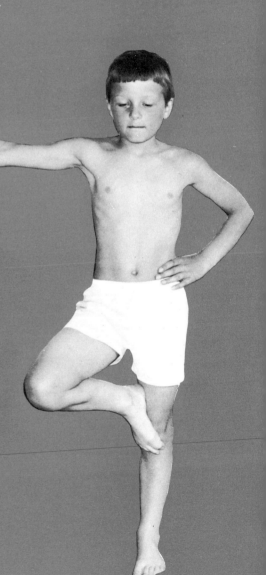

14.1

Running, leaping, showing first symmetrical and later asymmetrical positions in flight

Similar work in series 4, 9 and 10

Purpose

Concepts of symmetry and asymmetry as applied to body shape.

Teaching points

Whatever position you show in flight, get your feet together before landing.

Squashy landing.

Symmetry may be obtained with limbs in matching positions

a to the right and left

b to the front and rear

c positions between **a** and **b**.

Notes

See figs. 55, 68, 69 and 72

It may well be necessary to explain symmetry in body shape. If so, use static positions, e.g. standing in position of attention; X or Y shaped standing.

When children are leaping, landing quality tends to suffer, since they are concentrating on flight position. Insist on good quality landing, bringing feet together to meet the floor. This is much more difficult from asymmetrical positions.

14.2

Single floor movement in a symmetrical body shape. Later, using asymmetrical shapes

Purpose

Concepts of symmetry in movement.

Teaching points

Positions during the symmetrical work might include, from previous experience, movements of the type of rolls, wheels and various jumps.

Notes

Children should be asked to experiment with these movements in forward, backward and sideways directions, using variations of speed and variations of level.

There may be the possibility of mathematical links at this point, e.g. cartwheel = rotational symmetry.

14.3

Single balance, showing symmetrical body position; later showing asymmetrical position

Purpose

Further experience of symmetry of body position. Application of balance principles.

Teaching points

Most balance positions tend to be symmetrical.

Symmetry is an aid to balance.

Why is this?

Is it more difficult to balance in an asymmetrical position?

Why is this?

Notes

See figs. 105 and 106

It is better not to specify a number of points and/or patches until the children have grasped the concept.

To obtain asymmetrical balance positions easily, in the first instance, ask children to move one body part when in a symmetrical position. Here again is a possible mathematical link, by considering the links between symmetry and balance.

fig. 105

14.4

Symmetrical movement into symmetrical balance positions

Later, asymmetrical movement into asymmetrical balance position.

Later, combinations of symmetrical and asymmetrical.

Purpose

Development of symmetry and asymmetry concepts in movement with application of balance principles.

Teaching points

Two children, each in an asymmetrical balance position, when linked, can produce an overall symmetrical shape.

Notes

This is best initiated from very simple positions – e.g. standing facing each other with hands joined.

This illustrates the principle which is reinforced as children are encouraged to experiment further.

fig. 106

14.5

In pairs, partner linked balances

To show overall symmetry and later asymmetry.

Purpose

Two halves concept of symmetry and asymmetry.

Notes

See figs 89 and 93

This may be done freely at first and later on a given number of points or patches.

14.6

In pairs, symmetrical (or asymmetrical) movement to symmetrical (or asymmetrical) linked balance.

Purpose

As **14.5**

Notes

Having worked out the details of the movement, children should be encouraged to synchronise their movements.

Apparatus

As many and varied pieces as possible. Climbing frame and/or other vertical surfaces fit well into this series.

14a

Movement of apparatus

Similar work in all series

14b

Individually; symmetrical movement to apparatus, followed by symmetrical balance on apparatus

or between apparatus and

a floor

b wall

c other piece of apparatus.

Later, use of asymmetry in the above situations.

Purpose

Extension of floorwork principles by use of differing planes and levels.

Notes

It is suggested that children should work on a given piece of apparatus on a rotation basis, rather than a free choice being given.

This is very much an exploratory activity. Children will need to experiment and perhaps need guidance regarding starting position and direction of approach to apparatus, otherwise chaos may result.

14c

In pairs; as for 14b

Purpose

Partner work on apparatus to extend the concepts.

Notes

This is an extension of the work done in **14.5** and **14.6**. It is better if the children start by deciding on the balance position they will use, and then fit an appropriate approach movement to it.

14d

Extension of 14b and c

These ideas, as in **14b** and **14c**, may now be extended almost indefinitely by increasing the number of movements to, on and away from the apparatus, and by increasing the number of balances included. Further work may be done by specifying the number of points of support for each balance; by asking for differing directions, levels and speeds of movement.

Notes

Do give children the opportunity to practise, polish and finally present a finished piece of work before asking them to produce something else.

Difference for its own sake is seldom very productive.

N.B. The work in this series could easily become very static, i.e. lacking in movement in terms of covering plenty of floor.

If your work shows signs of becoming static, do not hesitate to break into the theme and use some other material to promote large scale movement for a few minutes, and then return to the theme.

14e

Replacement of apparatus

Similar work in all series

Formative and corrective movement

Although the philosphy and methods of practice in physical education have changed, the needs of the children remain fairly constant. One of the objectives of educational gymnastics is to assist in the promotion of healthy and posturally sound growth. Movement patterns aimed towards this should therefore be included. If the teacher is well versed in anatomy, physiology and human kinetics, there is no doubt that he or she will guide the children into these movement patterns in a manner which is integral to the theme he is using, and probably on an individual basis.

If, on the other hand, the teacher is not knowledgeable in these particular areas, it is possible that this aspect of the work will be neglected. There is no doubt that if a child has an obvious case of flattening of the foot, or some other marked postural defect, he will be referred for treatment elsewhere, but one of the functions of any form of systematised physical education is to nip this type of thing in the bud, to correct it before it becomes permanent. This aspect of educational gymnastics is probably more important in the age group 5 to 9 years than at any other time.

The following formative and corrective movement patterns are, in our opinion, well worth regular inclusion in lessons, and we have indicated in the various series, points at which they might be included without too artificial a departure from the theme being explored. It may be that a particular teacher, with a particular class, might decide that the need is such that a few minutes of each lesson should be devoted to this type of movement over a period of time, as a separate and unconnected part of the lesson.

Movement to combat malposture of the foot

1 Walking on the outside border of the foot. See **fig. 107.**
2 Walking, taking the weight as far back on the heel as possible, with the feet pointing upward. In this movement children should be encouraged to get the angle of the foot to the floor at up to 45 degrees, with the toes pointing to the ceiling. See **fig. 108.**
3 Walking, with the weight taken as high on the toes as possible. See **fig. 109.**

N.B. When doing this, children are really walking on their toes. Very often when doing normal walking or running, children are asked to *walk on your toes,* when what the teacher really wants them to do is move with the weight on the balls of the feet. Therefore, be careful with choice of words, otherwise, having asked for toes and accepted balls of feet, you will still get them, when to do this type of work you really need toes.

4 Any type of repetitive jumping, e.g. skip jumping, provided the heels make no contact with the floor.
5 Fists and fans. Children sit on the floor with legs stretched. Ask them to make their hands into fists and fans alternately (fingers maximally stretched and parted). Once the pattern is established, ask them to make fists and fans with both hands and feet together. Many will find difficulty in fanning their toes, but it is the effort of trying which is important.

Movements to combat general malposture and immobility

1 All movements which cause the spine to be extended (arched) fully should be encouraged. The very best position for this is the crab or wrestler's bridge, in that this extends the whole length of the spine. In addition it has a good suppling effect on the shoulder girdle and the pelvic girdle.

2 All positions where the spine is fully flexed (bent) are good. Tightly curled positions are ideal for achieving this effect.

N.B. In preventive work, as apart from remedial, excessive use of either of the above on its own will probably create more problems than it solves. Always try to achieve a balance between the two, i.e. if a movement causing sustained and repeated extension is used, follow it with another where flexion is caused.

3 All climbing, hanging and heaving activities.

General

When planning lesson material, it should be borne in mind that the child, and therefore the subsequent adult, tends to be weak in the shoulders and arms, in comparison with the strength of the hips and legs. Everything done in the standing position tends to strengthen the lower part of the body. This aspect of strength is acquired largely through normal everyday activities, whereas upper body strength is acquired largely through more artificial situations, such as P.E. lessons. Any work which is done with the body-weight borne on the hands, which promotes upper body strength, should therefore be encouraged, and lessons should be planned with a view to creating situations where this will occur.

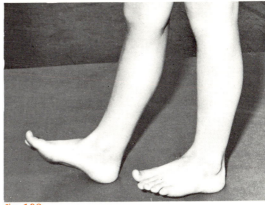

fig. 108

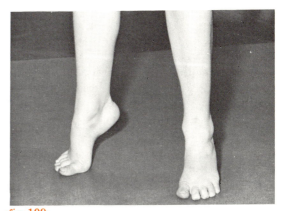

fig. 109

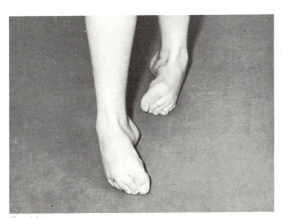

fig. 107

Techniques and teaching points

Handstanding activities
See figs. 10, 11, 12, 13, 14, 15, 17, 18, 105 and 110

This includes all the pre-handstanding activities, such as bunny jumps, kicking horses, etc. and applies to bent-legged and full handstands. The most important point of technique is that of pushing the head back on the neck. In a standing position, this would have the child looking at the ceiling. If the head is not well back when a child is on his hands, he will probably buckle and go right over on to his back.

Teaching points

Push your head back. It is as well to do this in the standing position first, to ensure that all the children understand what this means.
Look at the floor in front of you.
Look at my feet if the teacher is supporting the child.

fig. 110

See fig. 91. Children should be asked to recognise this as a strong position. With the head back, the position feels strong and secure, whereas with the head forward (chin on chest) it feels weak and insecure.

Once a child attempts something approaching a full handstand, he should be encouraged to turn his hands slightly inward, as this tends to keep the arms straight, and to work for a fully stretched position with legs and feet together and toes pointed.

Cartwheels
See figs. 53, 84 and 85

The early stage of teaching cartwheels is best done along a line. Lines marked on hall floors are ideal but in the absence of these, floor board edges can be utilised, especially when highlighted with chalk. In movement terminology, this is a hand – hand – foot – foot movement. Children should start in a star (or X) position, and attempt to hold this position all the way through the movement. They should be asked to work for a fully stretched position. As in handstanding, the head back position should be encouraged.

When working along a line, the first objective should be to get the hands coming down on to the line, one after the other, i.e. handstand. Having achieved this, children should be asked to try to get the first foot (and at a later stage the second foot as well) to land on the line. Once they have mastered the art of getting two hands and one foot on to the line they will not have a lot of trouble in getting the whole movement along the line.

A cartwheel is a useful activity, since a wide variety of movements may be created through incorporating the cartwheel movement, e.g.

Half cartwheel to handstand. This is a very slow movement, to stop in the upside down position and bring the legs together to the handstand position.
Half cartwheel down from handstand. In the handstand position, the legs are parted and the child comes to the floor as from a cartwheel.

Arab wheel. Start as for cartwheel, but bring the legs together as the movement passes through the upside down position. The child lands on two feet together, facing the way from which he has come. This in turn can lead into backward rolling activities.

Forward rolling activities
See figs. 47, 48 and 83

The tucked forward roll is the basis of all rolling activities in the forward direction, and, as the need arises, this should be taught.

Done badly, it is most uncomfortable for the child, and possibly dangerous, since if the child puts his head on the floor, there is a moment when all stress is taken by his bent neck. Done well, it is both aesthetically pleasing and a most useful safety measure, since many a bad landing has been made safe by a child's ability to forward roll out of it. In movement terminology, the body-weight is transferred from the feet to (in succession) feet and hands, hands, back of shoulders, back, seat, feet. At no point does the top of the head touch the floor or mat.

It is best to teach this from a standing position with feet apart. Children should be asked to bend forward, place hands flat on the floor, and look back through the legs. This latter ensures that the chin is on the chest, so that the next contact with the floor will be with the back of the shoulders. A light push off with the feet will initiate the roll into a sitting position. To complete the roll, to feet, the legs should be bent, knees to chest, immediately after the take-off, and, as the child gets on to his back, the arms should be stretched forward, as if reaching out for something. This will bring him to his feet. It is undesirable to teach, or allow children to push themselves to the final standing position. Should they do so, and fail to achieve the standing position, and start to fall back on to the mat, they could easily fall across the extended arm which is still in contact with the floor.

Forward rolling activities may be extended by variations to starting and finishing position, e.g. start with feet together, finish with feet wide apart. Possible sequence movements to and from rolling forward are,

bunny jump to forward roll
handstand into forward roll
headstand into forward roll
forward roll to headstand
forward roll, jump with half-turn backward roll
forward roll to bunny jump.

Backward rolling activities
See figs. 65 and 66

The tucked backward roll is the basis of all backward rolling activities, and for much the same reasons as for the basic forward roll, we feel it should be taught. In movement terminology, the body-weight is transferred from the feet to (in succession) feet and seat, lower back, upper back and hands, feet. The back of the head might touch the mat, but it bears no weight. It is best taught from a low crouch, back to the mat, with the hands, palms uppermost, resting on the shoulders, and the chin pressed well into the chest. At first, children should be encouraged to topple back on to the mat on to the back, until they can get the palms of the hands (which remain on shoulders) on to the mat. The main teaching point at this stage is, *keep curled up tightly*. When the children are able to do this with confidence, ask them to go back a little faster, and push as the hands contact the mat. Teaching points are *keep your chin on your chest* and *push hard with your hands*. The main fault, and it is this which causes most of the early failures, is not holding the tightly curled position throughout the movement.

The range of backward rolling movements may be extended by variations to starting and finishing positions. Some children, by timing the push of the hands, are able to push themselves through a near handstand position. Some very pleasing backward movements may be obtained by rolling over one shoulder rather than rolling straight backwards.

Headstanding activities
See figs. 22, 25 and 27

Children enjoy headstanding and it is another three-point balance that they can add to their achievements.

It is best taught with use of a mat, and children should be asked to kneel, with their hands flat on the floor, shoulder width apart, and place the forehead on the mat. Thus the two hands and the forehead form a triangle.

The teaching point, at this stage, is to ask the children to let the nose touch the mat. If they do not do so, they will transfer the weight from the relatively flat (stable base) forehead to the round (unstable base) top of the head as they lift their legs. From this starting position the next move is to walk the feet forward until they want to leave the floor, and at this point, lift both feet together to touch the heels to the bottom. This will give a tucked or curled headstand position, in which to balance. (**Fig. 22**)

Safety

In P.E., as in all other aspects of school life, the law requires us to take reasonable care for the children's safety. Reasonable care is defined as that which would be taken by a prudent parent. Additionally, the question 'Is it established or accepted practice?' has to be answered, in the event of litigation arising from an accident. The obvious implications of this lie in the realms of:

Supervision, which must be constant, and by qualified teachers. With regard to constancy of supervision it is apparent that a teacher will not leave a class unsupervised in a P.E. situation, but a less obvious lack of supervision might occur when a teacher is in a position relative to the class where he cannot see most, or many of them. This can happen when giving individual attention to a child, or a group. When doing this, the teacher should position himself so that he can look through the child, or group, at the hall as a whole. This normally means being positioned between the group and the wall, looking inward, rather than between the group and the centre of the hall, looking outward.

So far as qualification is concerned, it used to be very simple. The Teacher's Certificate specified to what extent, and with use of which apparatus, if any, that teacher was qualified to teach P.E. This practice has now ceased, and there seem to be no definitive sources of guidance regarding the current legal requirements in terms of qualification. In the absence of this, it has to be assumed that any possessor of a Teacher's Certificate is deemed to be a legally acceptable teacher of P.E. at First (or Infant and Junior) School level. The point of this would appear to be that if a person without a Teacher's Certificate is, for any reason, conducting a lesson in P.E., particularly with use of apparatus, the legal requirements are probably not being met. In such circumstances, the class teacher, or another qualified teacher, should be present to ensure that proper supervision is in force. Morally, as well as legally, the safety of the children must be our primary concern, and must take pride of place over any other consideration.

Proper and adequate supervision is very much dependent upon discipline. Different schools have different views on the type of discipline which is desirable, and on the methods to be used in obtaining it. Whichever type of discipline is recommended, however, it cannot be denied that unless children are willing to listen to what is being said to them and are willing to react in a desirable way to an instruction, a basic element of their education is being neglected, and no-one is going to be able to teach them anything. It can be said that if the disciplinary relationship between teacher and class is good, teaching has a chance to succeed. If it is not, teaching, no matter how good, has no chance at all. In educational gymnastics, as in all aspects of P.E., discipline is very much tied up with organisation, which includes lesson material, class and group working, and apparatus.

Organisation of lesson material. If the lesson is well planned so far as selection of activities is concerned, the lesson tends to flow well. The children will progress naturally and with an element of understanding from one activity to another, without the loss of concentration which a lesson made up of largely unconnected activities tends to produce.

Organisation of class and group working. When working on a class basis, with each individual using a certain amount of floor space, the nature of the activity should be considered before presenting it to the children. Collisions between children, even though not physically dangerous, tend to encourage some children to act in a silly way and attempt to cause more and greater collisions, which then might well become physically dangerous. Much, if not all, of this type of thing can be avoided if the teacher gives some thought as to how the particular activity should be organised. As teachers, we can usually predict how the children in our classes will react to a given situation. It seems, therefore, to be worth some thought to avoid creating situations from which loss of class control and danger might result.

We suggest, in the series plans, that groups should be on a permanent, or semi-permanent basis. This is a very similar situation to that of groups in a classroom; group co-ordination, etc. grows from the regularity of working with the same children. When group working becomes connected with apparatus handling, greater proficiency in safe and speedy handling will come through group co-operation. Group selection, as in the classroom, may be made on any one of a number of bases. For educational gymnastics, possible bases are ability, size, classroom groups, friendship, etc. With very young children, colour groupings are very useful, since this can contribute to many of the basic understandings which the teacher is attempting to inculcate in the classroom, e.g. *all the children in red shorts collect a red mat from the red corner.* The use of colour in this way must make some contribution to the mathematical concepts of sets and matching. Incidentally, this also applies with the many geometric shapes which are integral to educational gymnastics.

Organisation of apparatus. We consider that any apparatus which the children cannot themselves handle safely has no place in a school. We accept that this is very much an idealist view, when looked at in the context of financial stringency, schools being used for age groups other than those for whom they were originally designed, etc. It must be said, however, that unsuitable apparatus is one of the most important factors militating against good lesson planning.

We have suggested, from **series 1** onward, that the children should be trained in good apparatus handling procedures. This is important for both safety and efficiency. The safety aspect is largely negative, e.g. if apparatus is dragged instead of being lifted into position, it will score the floor, and children will get splinters sticking into them. If two children try to lift something that should be lifted by four, they will probably drop it, and perhaps injure themselves or someone else. The important thing is for the teacher to decide what is the best way to handle each piece, and how many children it needs to lift and carry it, and to train the children to do it in this way. Quite often, too many children trying to handle a piece will create as dangerous a situation as that which occurs with too few.

Four children tend to be the best number for most pieces of apparatus e.g. bench, large mat, trestle, ladder, etc.

In order to facilitate apparatus handling, the storage position for each piece should be considered relative to weight and shape, frequency of use, and, in some cases, distance from its best position in use. Great care should be taken when considering where to place each piece during the lesson. Wherever a landing is involved, the child should not land in proximity to a window, wall or other piece of apparatus. This is particularly difficult now that school halls have (rightly, in our opinion) taken on a more multi-purpose role. The hall should be the heart of a school, but it must be borne in mind that it is usually the only space where indoor P.E. lessons can be taken. Anything, therefore, which is placed in a school hall should be sited with the children's safety in mind. One sees so many potentially disastrous situations created by the installation in halls of trunk and face high shelves, units, trolleys, etc., usually with sharp corners. We feel that all indoor P.E. activities involving, as they do, physical movement, have sufficient inherent physical danger, and it is unfair to both the children and the teachers to introduce further hazards. When such facilities are being considered for a school hall, careful thought should be given to heights, placement, and so on. There is a legal phrase *res ipsa loquitur* (the thing speaks for itself) which is very apposite when thinking in terms of negligence regarding accidents arising from this type of situation.

Faulty apparatus

Faulty apparatus should be taken out of use immediately, and kept out of use until the necessary repair or replacement has been carried out. Knowing use of faulty apparatus is, in law, negligence. We are responsible for seeing that children are protected from their own tendency to act unwisely, therefore unserviceable apparatus should be made inaccessible to them.

Assisting and supporting

In days gone by, when a whole group, or even a whole class, lined up to take turns at some activity directed by the teacher, it was necessary for the teacher to know the classically correct method of support for the movements that he told the class to perform. Today, assistance and support is usually a matter of a child wishing to attempt a particular movement in response to the theme, and the teacher offering to help. It is important that this help should be offered, to enable children to master more difficult movements with an added degree of safety. The general principles for support and assistance for the most commonly used movements are as follows. Most activities in which a child will need assistance involve flight and a landing. Flight may be in the form of flight **on** to something, flight **off** something or flight **over** something, or any combination of these. Assistance for flight on is usually some form of lifting and steadying, as the child lands on the apparatus. Assistance is best given by the teacher positioning herself close beside the apparatus on the take-off side, facing the line of approach. She can then take the child's nearer arm, just above the elbow, and assist by lifting and holding the child until he has steadied in his landing position. For flight off, the teacher can best assist by standing facing the apparatus and the child, and catching the child by

the upper arms as he lands. This also applies to flight over.

If the child is attempting a movement whereby his leg (or legs) is carried out to the side in flight (e.g. leap frog), assistance should be given. The teacher should be on the landing side facing the apparatus and should lean forward across the apparatus to take the child by the upper arms.

Plate A Diagonal arrangement of apparatus

Plate B Balance and movements on points and patches